Writing
FAST

How to Write **Anything**
with Lightning Speed

jeff **bollow**

embryo films (publishing)

embryo films
(publishing division)
PO Box 68
St Pauls NSW 2031
Australia
embryo-films.com/publishing
writingFAST.com

First Edition

National Library of Australia Cataloguing-in-Publication Entry

Bollow, Jeff.
Writing FAST: how to write anything with lightning speed.

ISBN 0 9752139 0 3.

1. FAST (Writing system). 2. Writing. 3. Authorship.
4. Motion picture authorship. I. Title.

808.066

First printing (Limited Edition), May 2004
Second printing (First Edition), August 2004

Printed by Southwood Press
Manufactured in Australia

Writing FAST

for those who see beyond
what is already here

may this help you show us
what you see

Thank-you

To Missi, for your incredible support and encouragement, and for your love; you are a truly beautiful person.

To Dad, for your patience and belief, and for your friendship; it helps in ways that even "fast" words can't describe.

To my students, for teaching me more than I ever taught you; please get off your butts and apply this stuff.

And to you, the reader, for taking this plunge; you make my efforts worthwhile.

Table of Contents

66 We are what we repeatedly do.
Excellence then, is not an act,
but a habit. **99**

—Aristotle

Introduction

There's only one reason I've written this book. And it's found within this introduction. If you don't grasp that reason, you'll still be able to use the FAST System to write anything with lightning speed.

But you'll miss the whole point of the book.

So I'd ask you — please — to read the introduction. Every story needs a context. This is the context for the FAST System.

And I promise you this: The FAST System, when properly understood and applied, will revolutionize the way you write. It's simple, it's effective, and it works.

But I never wanted to write it.

What Are You Talking About?

In fact, if you had told me just *one* year ago that I'd be writing this book (and writing it in 8 weeks, no less!), I would have laughed. And probably walked away from you.

A year ago, I was disillusioned. I had become something I specifically did not want to become. I had become a respected and highly-regarded screenwriting teacher. Or, as one of my students put it: "the screenwriting guy."

God I hate that.

Don't get me wrong. I love screenwriting, and I actually enjoy teaching the stuff. I don't even have a problem with screenwriting teachers in general. It's a valid career, and it's certainly necessary. (I wish they had a better grasp of what they were teaching sometimes, but what can ya do?)

But I wasn't "the screenwriting guy." Was not. *Am* not.

I'm just a guy with a vision. And it can't be built without dozens (probably hundreds) of excellent screenplays.

I'm a guy on the prowl, looking for scripts.

See, I want to build an independent feature film studio, and produce 3 to 6 movies per year. All kinds of movies. And I want to build it from the ground up. To prove it can be done.

So when I couldn't find any screenplays (any commercially-viable ones, anyway), I did whatever I could think of to get people writing them. Taught workshops. Imported software. Assessed scripts. Mentored writers. Everything. I created Screenplay.com.au.

But I never considered myself a writer. I'd write if I had to, but I *make* movies. I always found the *writing* part torturous. But movies don't get made without screenplays, so I need writers. Back to square one.

In my hometown of L.A., everyone's got a screenplay tucked under their arm. Even the waiters. *Especially* the waiters. You can go to lunch at Denny's and feel like you're right in the middle of the studio system.

But when I moved to Australia, I found a very different landscape. Not only were the waiters really waiters, no one else seemed to be writing any screenplays either.

So I did what any self-respecting producer would do.

I tried to corner the market on screenwriting.

A Brilliant I...dea

Tell me this isn't a great idea: I would develop a workshop to teach emerging writers how to write commercially-viable screenplays — from the producer's perspective. Marketable screenplays producers would actually want to buy.

And because I'm a producer who's been through the entire process myself — from start to finish — I'd show my students what really works and what really doesn't. And then, naturally, I'd be the first producer they'd turn to when they finished their screenplay.

Not a bad idea, right?

Well, yeah, in theory. In practice, something else happened. I unwittingly started a new career.

It began with an eight-week *First Draft Workshop* designed to take writers "from concept to completion." But I quickly realized that my students didn't even know the fundamentals. Eight weeks was just too quick. We needed more time for the basics.

So I pulled the workshop apart, and created a weekend workshop to cover the fundamentals: *The Essential Screenwriting Workshop* would be "everything you need to know *before* you write your screenplay." And a prelude to the eight-weeker.

I planned to run them until I found a core group of writers who wanted to join me, and churn out material I could produce.

Cut to four years later.

I had done 56 weekend workshops with 641 participants, aged 15 to 72, in six cities across Australia and New Zealand. I had spent over $100,000, barely made a subsistence income, and put up to 80 hours a week into them.

And nearly 100% of participants raved about the workshops. They said they would "enthusiastically recommend" them. I was very proud.

But a pattern had emerged.

As it turned out, less than 5% of participants actually *did* anything with the information. Less than 5% wrote anything at all. 95% of my effort was being wasted.

Dazed and Confused

These were good, intelligent people. From all backgrounds and levels. Smart people. I knew I could share this alarming fact with them. So I would say, "Statistically, I will only hear from two of you ever again." In one workshop, a woman raised her hand and replied, "I'd like to know who the *other* one is."

The class laughed.

And I never heard from her again.

Why? Why was this happening? I had become a screenwriting teacher. I had taken my attention away from getting films produced. And I had *nothing* to show for it. I needed to find out why. So I asked my students.

And overwhelmingly, the response I got was this: "Things keep coming up." "I'm too busy." "Writing a screenplay is a huge project, and I don't have the time to get through it."

Let me say this right now. If you don't write, you'll never get better at it. Practice makes perfect. So if you don't *make* time to write, how can you get good enough to sell your work?

And (more importantly to me) how will I ever get enough screenplays to achieve my vision?!

I remembered my favorite quote from the late great acting teacher, Sanford Meisner. It goes like this:

"That which hinders your task *is* your task."

So if no one has time to write, that's what I've got to do. Show them a way to write, even if they don't have time.

A Whole New Approach

So the first thing I did was fall out of a plane.

January 2nd, 2004. My first freefall.

There's something about skydiving that's simply electrifying. It's life on the edge. It's fast. It's extreme. And, for me at least, it shocked my senses back into focus.

Within a week, my life suddenly made sense again.

I had gone on a four-year detour. It was time to put my workshops into a box. A box I could offer to the serious students.

That way, I could continue "teaching," and still get back to making films. And if only 5% of readers ever applied it, I'd still be moving forward. No time would be wasted.

But if I was going to put my workshops in a box, it had to be perfectly clear, and it needed to obliterate this time problem.

And then it hit me.

The reason was obvious! My students loved the workshops, but didn't do anything with it. Why? They didn't have a *system* for applying it. I had given them tons of valuable information — practical stuff they could use immediately — but they didn't walk away with a system for *writing*. A system that works.

So I would develop one. I wanted something that would help people beat the time crunch. Something that would help them write fast.

That was it! FAST. F.A.S.T. What a perfect acronym to describe what we're trying to do. You want to *write* fast. I want to *read* fast. Writing is a four-part process, and the letters fit the four parts perfectly...

You'd laugh if you knew how excited I got. Suddenly the world made sense. Finally, I could help writers master this seemingly impossible craft. And in the process, I could get you writing screenplays I could produce.

Fantastic.

The Whole World Sings

I mapped out this workshop-in-a-box, and I called it FASTscreenplay. It would be a step-by-step approach to *writing* a screenplay. It wouldn't be about formulaic plots, or "write-like-this" rules. No. I've met enough writers and read enough screenplays to know that no "formula" really works.

Instead, FASTscreenplay would be a system for *writing* a screenplay. You'd power through your script, blasting past the time problem, creating a compelling *original* screenplay.

When I finished mapping it out, I noticed something. Ironically, I was *using* the FAST System to create FASTscreenplay.

It dawned on me: The FAST System works across the board!

Not just screenwriting, but *all* forms of writing. And when I looked closer at it, it made perfect sense. It's a systematic approach to *writing*.

And then I thought about Australia's armpits. And, specifically, how none of them were carrying any screenplays. How, in fact, embarrassingly few Australian writers have even considered screenwriting. Many don't even know what it is, or what it looks like.

What if — instead — I wrote a book about the FAST System in general (as it applies to *any* kind of writing)? I could kill two birds with one stone.

I could show you how to write *anything* faster and better. And at the same time, I could reach a much wider audience. Sooner or later, I'm bound to bump into a would-be screenwriter, right?

And that brings us to *Writing FAST*. I have ulterior motives here. I'm not looking to start a new career on the lecture circuit. And I don't want to become a guru.

I want you to use the FAST System for whatever you want to write.

But I'm secretly hoping you'll write screenplays.

What's Inside (and What's Not Inside)

Now, before we leap into it, I need to clarify a couple things.

Writing FAST is not about grammar and tense and viewpoint and punctuation. We'll get into some of that in the Tweak section, but this book assumes you have a decent understanding of the English language.

If you don't, you *must* learn that stuff. Effective writing isn't filled with typos and errors and point-of-view mistakes. There's no shame in not knowing it. But when you discover you don't know it, it's time to learn.

There are dozens of books on the subject. You don't need to read them now, but don't avoid them afterwards. Writing is about communicating your ideas. And the better you understand your language, the better you can use it.

Writing FAST is also not about speed writing. We do cover it (in detail), but it's only one part of the FAST System (the Apply section). And it's not even the most important thing. FAST is an approach to the whole process. Speed writing is only one fourth of the equation.

And I'm not going to make ridiculous promises. Can you write a book in 2 weeks, or 4 weeks, like some speed writing advocates claim? Maybe you *can*. Maybe you can write even faster! But I don't know you. I have no idea what your natural abilities are. So I refuse to make such blanket promises.

What's more important to me is that your work *reads* fast. Clunky, cumbersome writing is a chore to read, no matter how fast you wrote it. The Tweak Section will certainly help (a lot!). But it, too, takes practice. Just remember. It's not a race with anyone else. Life is a race with yourself.

Writing FAST is a simple, step-by-step approach to the process of writing. I want to give you a way to smash the time barrier, so you never have an excuse for not writing again.

I say that *Writing FAST* will help you write ten times as fast as you do right now. If you truly apply it, you'll do a lot better than that. And I can't wait to hear your feedback when you do.

You're gonna have so much fun.

Ready to get started?

[The Setup]

❝ Nothing leads so straight to futility
as literary ambitions without
systematic knowledge. **❞**

—H.G. Wells

1

Why Write FAST?

The written word started out as a picture.

Way back in prehistoric times, life was slow. People would hunt and gather all day, and then come home to the cave and grunt at each other around the campfire. There wasn't a whole lot of reading and writing going on — fast or otherwise.

But one day (and I'm taking a little "creative license" here), some guy named Ooga saw a mammoth for the first time. It scared the crap out of him. He ran back to the cave to warn his friends (let's call them Booga and Shooga), but they just scratched their heads. Booga and Shooga had never seen a mammoth before, so Ooga's frantic grunting wasn't making any sense. (Maybe they should take him out back, and club him for awhile?)

But Ooga was serious. That hairy, oversized elephant was huge. With tusks and everything. It could kill them! He needed his friends to understand. But he didn't have the right grunt to describe it. So he grabbed a piece of tree bark, and drew a picture of the mammoth on the wall.

After Booga freaked out (grunting angrily about vandalism and such), Shooga grabbed his arm. She sat him down and made him stare at Ooga's crude drawing. And, gradually, the image of the mammoth filled their minds. They understood.

And written communication was born.

Today, some thirty-five thousand years later, we communicate with different kinds of pictures. Our pictures are drawn with words. With words, we can create images of incredible subtlety and complexity. For example, I just painted the image of some cavemen, their cave drawings, and even a glimpse of their social structure, without any graphics at all.

And, just like Booga and Shooga, you saw that scene in your mind's eye. You saw the mammoth.

Writing is communicating your idea with the written word.

And writing FAST is doing it quickly and effectively.

What's In Store For You in this Book

This book will teach you how to write fast.

Not just speed writing techniques (although there are some whoppers in here). But also techniques for nailing your idea. Figuring out exactly what you're trying to say, and then giving you a razor-sharp plan to get there.

This book will give you a system. One that works for *any* kind of writing. It's a system that — when you fully understand it — will make writing simple. You'll even have a two-minute checklist to immediately break down even the most complex writing projects. And an easy acronym to remember it by.

This book is not about me. Writing is *never* about the author. This book is about *you*. I want you to understand this system. I want you to see how it works. And I want you to be able to use it. To apply it. Immediately.

If you've looked at the Table of Contents, you already know the "big picture." But we're about to go way deeper.

With FAST, you can break down any complex writing job — from thousand-page novels and screenplays to simple letters and emails — and write them faster than you ever imagined possible.

This book will go beyond just the four-part process of writing. We'll look at specific tips, techniques and methods to make sure you not only write *faster* than ever before, but *better*, as well.

We'll look at things like "chunking," which simplifies the huge task of long-form writing. I'll introduce you to Talktation, my brand new technique for speed writing. You'll discover the Stack Test, and watch it lift the quality of your work. And you'll find dozens of ways to "speed up" your writing, so your reader hangs on every word, and can't turn away.

If I do my job right, you'll breeze through this book. It should be a quick and easy read. And with any luck, ideas will be popping into your head on every page.

To make it easy, this book is broken down into six sections.

First is The Setup. Every word you write falls into one of two categories — Setup or Payoff — so I've included them as sections, to remind you. All ideas need a context, or they won't be understood. The setup gives us that context. (In the caveman story, the "Way back..." paragraph is the setup.)

Next are sections for each of the four parts of the FAST System itself: F(ocus), A(pply), S(trengthen), T(weak). That's the meat of the system. You'll spend varying amounts of time on each part of the process, as you need to. But do each part in that order. You only struggle when you jump around.

The final section shows you how to apply it: The Payoff. The payoff is where an idea becomes clear and usable. It's when you go "Ah!" The payoff is what all writing is really about. (See if you can identify the Payoff in the caveman story, and I'll tell you if you're right a little later.)

What's In Store When You're Done

When you're done with this book, you'll write ten times faster than you ever did before. You'll write with lightning speed — the speed of thought. And I'm completely and totally serious.

Here's how it'll work:

An idea will pop into your head. Maybe it's a book, a novel, screenplay, article, report... whatever. Within a few short hours (for the long stuff) or just a few minutes (for the short stuff), you'll know exactly what to write on every single page.

Then you'll write it. And I mean fast. It's so easy, in fact, you'll be amazed. It's as if the book is just flowing out of you.

Then you'll inspect what you've written. Here's where most speed writing techniques fail, and most writers get discouraged. But not with FAST. As you read your work, you'll immediately spot dazzling ways to transform it into gold. Problems leap out. And the solutions are crystal clear.

And finally, almost as if you've got magic fingers, you'll sift through your work... twisting, tugging, and straightening out every kink, and making your writing electrifying.

You'll complete your book (or whatever you're writing) in record time, impressing everyone you know (especially yourself!).

Readers will love it. You'll grab them with your style, and they'll hang on every word. You'll be writing *fast* in every sense.

That's what's in store for you when you finish this book.

No more writers block. Ever.

No more battling with Time. You'll have a system for writing, even if you can only squeeze in twenty minutes a day.

No more getting intimidated by big projects. You'll wonder how they ever scared you in the first place.

No more tired, boring, bloated writing. You'll keep your reader glued.

I want you to get excited. I want you to read this book from cover to cover as quickly as possible, and then refer to it later when you need to. Because as soon as you're done, you're going to reach lightning speeds. Almost as fast as you can think.

What Do You Want to Write?

To get an idea of just how powerful this FAST System really is, let's rattle off some of the things you can write with it.

A screenplay. A novel. A non-fiction book. A textbook. A technical book. A magazine article. A news story. A television show. An essay. A dissertation. A homework assignment. An autobiography. Somebody else's biography. A report. A business plan. A website. A proposal. A journal. A travelogue. A diary. A short story. A novella. A bible. A procedure book. A brochure. An advertisement. A manual. A pamphlet. An email. A play. A critique. A letter. A white paper. A manifesto. A handbook. A newsletter. A bulletin. A query. A review...

I'm sure there are a hundred more, but you get the idea.

You'll use the FAST System to write every single one of these. In fact, here's a secret I'll get to in a minute: You *must* use a system to write *any* of them! That's why the FAST System is such a breakthrough. It harnesses the power of your mind.

Each type of writing has its own purpose. So, what makes good screenwriting is different to what makes good novel writing. But the approach is identical. They're all communication, and that's what this book is all about.

Think about what you want to write. Is it a book? A novel? A personal newsletter? A screenplay?

Pick one. Right now. And hold onto it.

Having an example project as you read through this book will help you visualize each step. It'll make it more practical.

Apply everything you learn to your example. And watch as it unfolds before your eyes.

Writing FAST Versus Writing Slow

Here's the first major lesson: Writing is not an activity. It's not something you sit down at the keyboard, and just start doing. That's called "typing."

Typing is an activity. Scribbling words onto paper is an activity. Dictating into a microphone is an activity.

Writing is *not* an activity.

Writing is a *process*. And if you start thinking of it as a process, life gets so much easier.

Here's how it works. You have an idea. You want to express it on the page. You use the *process* of writing to say it in the most effective way possible.

The difference between writing *fast* and writing *slow* is how fast the idea pours out of you. (Simple enough.) But understand this: When you write slow, you're over-analyzing. You're jumping ahead in the process. You're stifling your own idea!

On the other hand, when you write *fast*, you're tapping into your idea, and letting it spill out onto the page. You're *using* the process to work its magic. You're trusting the outcome.

The FAST System helps you write *fast*. It helps you discover, understand, and shape your idea. It provides techniques to get your ideas on the page faster. And it makes sure your idea is expressed as perfectly as possible.

If you've been writing without a system, you've been spinning your wheels. You've been keeping yourself busy with an activity. It's time to try the process.

Couldn't Possibly Be Me

If you're new to writing, you might have writophobia. (Yes, I just made up a word.) I used to have it, too. It's when "real" writers scare the bejeezus out of you.

I never expected to write professionally. At first, I was intimidated by writers, just like you are. I had an image in my head of exactly what a writer looks like. And it certainly wasn't me.

You know the image. It's that guy in the log cabin on that sprawling wooded property in the mountains. The one with no television set, and seven hundred hardcover books on crowded little bookshelves. The guy with the beard, who wears glasses (but only when he's reading), and is probably too smart to have a normal conversation with. (Aw, let's face it, he's Stephen King.)

Anyway, after four years of teaching screenwriting, my writo-phobia disappeared. How? I met people who write. In four years, I met over six hundred writing students. And I can tell you this. Maybe three of them fit that image. The rest looked like everyone else in the world.

But here's the kicker. I also taught professional writers — people with film credits, published novels, journalists, magazine columnists, playwrights — they were just like everyone else, too!

The entire mystique of writing fades away when you get a load of who does this stuff.

We're all people. We all have the same potential.

So if you're a novice, know this: All you need to do is apply the FAST System, and practice. Good writing is good writing. It's not the exclusive domain of some mysterious aristocracy.

And if you're a professional, you already have the discipline it takes to sit in a chair for extended periods of time. Now you'll accomplish twice as much, with less time in the chair. (And that's being conservative!)

See, writing is writing. Wherever you are on the food chain, it's all the same. A systematic approach will get you there faster.

Even if you're Stephen King.

(Although from what I hear, he's already lightning fast.)

The Battle for Time

Now usually, it's just an excuse. But one of the biggest reasons students give for not writing is a lack of time. You lead a busy life. You've got a career with business trips and meetings. Or maybe you've got two jobs and three kids. Or perhaps it's a full schedule of classes and homework with a part-time job.

Look around. We're all busy. We watch days, weeks, months, and years go by without achieving the things we had resolved to achieve at the start of the year.

If you need eight hours a day for six months straight to write your book, it's just not gonna happen. A screenplay isn't guaranteed income, so the kids come first. A report isn't urgent, so it gets pushed down the To-Do list. The newsletter won't be done this month because of the sales meeting. And so on.

And when these things happen, you feel a tremendous sense of frustration. Even guilt. Sometimes stress. You know it, I know it. You can't get out from under it and it drives you crazy.

In a way, the FAST System is a time-management technique. I was tired of hearing my students say they didn't have enough time. (I was tired of not having enough time myself!)

Even if you only have ten minutes a day to write (which is never *really* the case, but let's go with it), the FAST System will help you. In fact, if you really tuck into it, amazing things are possible. What if you could write a book in just a few months, using the FAST System on ten minutes a day? Some readers will. It might take practice, but wouldn't it be worth it?

Your Chance to Change the World

Now this might sound corny, but I believe you're capable of more than you imagine. And I think every last one of us has at least one unique, major, world-changing idea inside us. And if we don't reveal it in our lifetime, it gets lost forever.

For example, mine might be the FAST System. (I think I've got a couple more, but I'll save them for another time.)

FAST is a lucky discovery. If I had made *one* different choice at *any* point along the way, I wouldn't be writing this book.

And if I didn't, some of my readers might never muster the confidence to write theirs.

It's a chain effect. My ideas help spark your ideas. Your ideas will help spark someone else's ideas.

Let's take an imaginary chain.

Suppose a businessman makes a startling discovery about how his customers interact. Until FAST, he could never find time to write a book about his discovery. But now he can. He does.

Meanwhile, a scientist is working on a life-saving drug. He's never heard of FAST, but he reads the businessman's book. And it sparks an idea: "What if the *chemicals* in this drug interacted the same way those customers did?" Suddenly, he solves a riddle he's been working on for five years. He writes a breakthrough white paper on how to cure this rare disease.

A doctor in a remote country town reads the white paper. He has just delivered a child who happens to have the rare disease. The doctor would've misdiagnosed it just six months before. But now he can treat the child easily. And a young couple will see their daughter grow into an Olympic medalist.

This isn't fiction. It's an imaginary scenario, but that's exactly the kind of sequence life takes. That's exactly how knowledge builds. Ideas spark ideas.

And if you follow this logic, I believe it's vitally important that *you* share your own life's discoveries. No matter how inconsequential they seem to you, they could spark an idea in someone else — something you couldn't possibly imagine. The businessman in our example could never predict that his book would be responsible for solving the riddle of a life-saving drug. The businessman knows nothing about biochemistry. He only knows about his customers' interactions.

But where does that spark lead?

Where does *your* spark lead?

Will you let this book spark you?

It's All Communication

There's a myth that's been passed down from generation to generation. And I have to admit, it's tempting to continue that tradition. Catch me at the wrong moment, in fact, and I will.

The myth is that writing is hard work. That it's something only a very special kind of person can do.

Writers throughout the ages have promoted that myth (some even believe it), because it helps their mystique. Think about it. What kind of reaction do you get if you're sitting next to someone on a plane, and when they ask what you do, you hand them your book?

What's the reaction? It's magical, isn't it? Suddenly, they're in awe. There's a reverence for you. You're a writer. That's something they could never do!

Or so they think. (And you probably *let* them think it, too!)

C'mon. That's ridiculous.

Not only can anyone do it, I believe everyone *should* do it.

Writing is not the mythical realm of the gods. Writing is really very simple. It's effective communication. It's putting your ideas into words that will be clear in a distant time and place. Nothing more.

It takes time to learn. (What doesn't?) It takes practice to get good at. (What doesn't?) But if *I* can do it, *you* can do it. And the passenger next to you can do it, too.

Short-form writing (a letter, email, web page, short story) has a quick point. Long-form writing (a book, novel, screenplay) has a more elaborate point, or more layers and depth. Large ideas will take planning and organization.

For example, I can communicate FAST (Focus, Apply, Strengthen, Tweak) in four words. But the depth and breadth of the idea — the detail you'll need to use it effectively — takes quite a bit longer to express. I'm using eighteen chapters.

But it's all communication. I can do it fast, or I can do it slow. And so can you.

Simplifying the Complex

The real problem is that you have a million possible choices. And there's virtually no way to know which one's "right."

I believe this chapter will put you in the right frame of mind to understand the FAST System. I think it'll be a useful framework for you. (And when I re-read it later, if I think I was wrong, I'll adjust it. [Which I just did.])

But I could put a nearly infinite combination of words on this page right now to express this idea. Which one's right? Which one's better than all the rest? Which one's wrong?

Truth is, you're looking in the wrong place. There *is* no "right" or "wrong." There are only varying degrees of effectiveness. And that's what makes writing so incredibly challenging.

(Which fosters the myth that writers are so mysterious.)

When you read a published book (a good one, anyway), it's well-written. It's clever. Concise. Simple. It looks like the writer did it effortlessly. You think to yourself, *I could never do that.*

But why not? It's only a matter of communicating. Of turning the ideas in your head, into words on a page. And making sure the idea is as dynamic on the page as it was in your head.

Enter the FAST System.

Suddenly, the process is simple. FAST walks you step-by-step through it. It breaks it down into manageable pieces. It keeps you from getting lost. And that's its power.

To all the writers out there who promote the mystique that writing is hard, I formally apologize for ruining it for you.

But I believe that every one of us has something to share, and if a writer doesn't share it, I (personally) might miss out on the chain effect of their spark. And what if it's something that could change or save my life?

I want you to write. And because I want that, I'm going to show you how to take what appears to be a complex process, and make it simple, fast, effective and fun!

That's how the chain works.

And so...

Writing is a process, and without a simple, step-by-step approach to that process, you're creating unnecessary work for yourself. Why struggle with something that should be easy?

In this chapter, I've tried to put you in the right frame of mind, to get the most out of this system. Remember, every idea needs a context. And that's what this chapter is all about.

For FAST, the context is this: *All writing is communication.* It's so easy to get lost when your idea could go in any one of a million different directions. By applying the FAST System, you put yourself on a clear, simple road.

And it's right there to help you, during each of the most challenging phases of writing. It will help you, stabilize you, and get you back on track, every step of the way.

And your results will be startling.

You'll nail down your idea in record time. You'll blast through the writing. You'll quickly spot problems and know exactly how to fix them. And then you'll turn it all into a lightning-fast read.

If you're not excited yet, don't worry. I'm excited enough for the both of us. Because I know what's in store for you when you're done with this book.

Sure, you'll know how to write FAST.

But more importantly, you'll discover your spark.

2 Why You Hate Writing

I guarantee you, someone out there got this book, reached this chapter, shook her head and frowned. Then she smiled (almost laughing at the rest of us), and thought to herself, *I don't hate writing. I LOVE writing!*

If that person is you, please forgive me. I've got to talk to the rest of the readers for a chapter. The 90% of people who (like me) have always felt that writing is agony. You can still read along, and see what mere mortals go through. But please sit quietly, and don't snicker.

Now then, back to you. Pay no attention to her. She's probably off doing some creative writing exercise anyway. We're alone now, and we can talk about the truth of this writing crap.

You hate it, don't you? Yeah, I feel your pain.

There's nothing worse than knowing you have to plant your butt in that chair and pound furiously at the keyboard for hours on end, thinking the whole time that your work is probably going to be terrible, and another day "writing" will have been wasted.

I know you want to give up. I know you want to chuck the computer out the window. I know you want to scream at the top of your lungs sometimes.

I know.

And that's why I decided to take this chapter and explain exactly why you hate it so much. Why it's so frustrating.

And how to beat it.

Because once you see *why* you hate it, you'll begin to see

exactly what you're doing wrong.

And then, best case scenario, you'll be as excited about your writing as our snickering friend.

Or the worst-case scenario, you can get through the writing you've just gotta get through.

Like I am now.

It's Okay, You Can Admit It

It's probably sacrilegious to talk about what a terrible, evil thing writing is. Especially in a book *about* writing. After all, kids might be reading this. We don't want them to think writing's so awful, do we?

Too bad. The first step in your road to recovery is to understand that we all hate writing. Even that goody-goody from the previous segment hates it (although she'd never admit it). She might not hate is as *often* as you or I do, but you'd better believe she's got her moments.

You're not alone.

To one degree or another, we all hate writing because we all get frustrated by it. In truth, it's more of a love/hate relationship. We love it when we write something that rocks. But we hate it when our writing is atrocious.

And since it seems to be atrocious more often than not, we hate it more often than we love it.

The trouble is that writing is difficult to grasp. It's amorphous. You can't touch it. Or feel it. There are no boundaries or edges to it. You can't put it in a box.

It's a giant, shapeless void that doesn't exist until it's already done. And you can't hold it up and say, "this is my writing."

Oh, sure, you can hold up pages with words on them. But that's just words on pages. That's not your writing. Your writing is the effect and the totality of your expression.

The only way someone can *see* your writing is by actively engaging it. By *reading* it. You can't point to your writing from across the room. You can only point to the *shape* of your writing — the book, the magazine article, the letter.

What this means is that writing has no single result. It does not have a specific, logical outcome, like a mathematical equation would have. It's all fuzzy. It's all aesthetic. Even two professional editors at major publishing houses would edit this very manuscript in completely different ways.

But there's no "right" way to do it. Sure, you can be grammatically correct enough to impress your English teacher, but then a book like *Trainspotting* comes along, and offers a new "right" way. What about that? Hmm?

And since there's no "right" way, there also can't be a "wrong" way. So how do you know if yours is any good or not? You use the same gauge most writers use. You end up comparing your writing to what you've read elsewhere.

And that can be a killer.

Excuses, Excuses

When you're afraid your work won't hold up to comparison, what's the first thing you do? Write? Of course not. The first thing you do is make excuses.

And don't tell me you don't. I know you do. I hear excuses every time I ask my students how their writing is going.

One of the biggest excuses is some form of the "I'm not good enough" category. You don't write because you're convinced your writing isn't ready for prime time.

Maybe you've got a favorite author whose words you compare yours to. The guy has probably been writing for thirty years, but if the first few sentences you plop on the page aren't as good as his, you're immediately certain there's no hope for you.

Let me say right now, you *are* good enough. And you'll be even better when you stop comparing your work to other writers. We'll get to more of this idea later on.

Another major excuse is the time thing. You don't have time. You just moved house. You're studying for your PhD. You just got married. Or divorced. You had kids. You changed jobs. You moved to another city. You've been away on business. You've had to look after a sick relative. You've had to fulfill your duties as mayor. Whatever.

Believe it or not, that's just your way of avoiding it. The busiest person in the world still needs to eat, sleep and... do other things. You could steal an extra twenty minutes a day if you wanted to. And I'll show you how to use those twenty minutes most effectively in the coming chapters.

Then there's the "nothing to say" excuse. You don't think you've got anything to write about. But your road is unique. You've got *plenty* to write about! Even if someone else has already written about it, your voice is original. Add your spark!

How about the "I'm overwhelmed by it" excuse? You know. "A screenplay is too big a project." "I don't think I'm ready for that." Bah humbug! It may be true, but to use it as an excuse for not writing is weak and spineless. Just write it! If it's terrible, you'll learn something, and your next one will be better.

Or the "writing is boring" excuse. You get fidgety. You find it tedious. Your brain goes numb when you attempt it. I won't say too much about this excuse, because when you've finished this book, you'll never even think this one again.

Excuses all come from the same place. You make excuses when you're scared. When you're convinced your writing is terrible. When you think you'll be wasting your time by doing it.

The remedy isn't where you think it is. You're looking in the wrong place. Where you need to look, instead, is inside your brain.

Meet Your Brain

As a writer, it helps to understand this grey matter inside your skull. After all, it's your single most important tool, right?

Now, technically, scientists are already discovering that what I'm about to say isn't quite right. But for our purposes, it's the perfect analogy. And it's a great way to understand why you hate writing so much. So I'm using it. Science be damned.

In simplistic terms, your brain has two sides.

The Right-brain and the Left-brain.

The Right-brain is the creative, intuitive, free-thinking, artistic side of your brain. Your Right-brain is the side that plays the guitar and thinks about art, and comes up with crazy ideas and has lots of "hunches." It even drives your car for you, until you suddenly snap out of your trance and realize you can't remember driving those past ten minutes.

The Left-brain is the side that snapped you out of it.

The Left-brain is the analytical, logical, problem-solving, scientific side of the brain. Your Left-brain is the side that organizes your desk and plans your day, and decides you'd better not have that extra piece of chocolate. It does the math and keeps you from making a total fool of yourself in public (mostly).

Everyone has (and needs) both sides. Some people may tend toward one or the other, but both sides work their magic at all times. It's an elaborate dance of give-and-take.

But can you see the problem for writers?

The problem is that both sides are always dancing with each other. Interfering. And writing demands the effective use of *both* sides of your brain. Not just one. Both. Each side in turn.

And the reason you hate writing so much is because you start analyzing your work before you're done pouring it onto the page. Your Left-brain won't let your Right-brain do its job.

That may work well for daily living, but it's a killer for your writing. Because you can't write effectively without giving both sides their chance to shine.

Your Right-brain gets the words on the page. The Left-brain makes them sing.

Everybody's a Critic

Since I'm a movie guy, I have another analogy.

I call them the Oscar-winner and the Movie Critic.

Tell me if you recognize this scenario.

One day, you have a brilliant idea for a story (a screenplay, a novel, whatever). You love it. It's fantastic! This may be the best idea you've ever had in your whole life.

Inside your mind, there's this little voice. I call him the Oscar-winner. And every time you come up with an idea, the Oscar-winner inside your mind goes nuts. He loves it. He thinks it's the best idea since canned tuna. (He thinks your movie idea is going to win him an Oscar, see. Hence his name.)

But the problem is that the Oscar-winner loves *every* idea you come up with. Just the fact that you *have* an idea, sends the Oscar-winner into fits of hysteria. This idea is amazing! I'm so totally *pumped* about this one! This one's going all the way!!!

And then you start writing.

And then you notice the other voice inside your head. I call him the Movie Critic. He starts looking over what you've written. But he's a critic, so he starts pointing out all its flaws and imperfections.

Which *can* be a good thing. You don't want to send your work out flawed, right?

But this voice isn't like a real movie critic. This one criticizes *everything*. He doesn't offer a balanced review. He just shreds everything. "This is terrible." "That's horrible." "That over there is downright embarrassing."

And before you know it, you've stopped writing, because the Movie Critic has quashed the Oscar-winner's enthusiasm. (Now he can't even *imagine* winning an Oscar. ...What, with *that* crap?)

You hate writing because you're judging yourself every step of the way. The Oscar-winner is the Right-brain. The Movie Critic is the Left-brain. You need both. You couldn't write your project on the enthusiasm of the Movie Critic. And you couldn't objectively judge your project on the critique of the Oscar-winner.

If you can recognize those two voices in your mind, you can give each their time in the spotlight. And you can yank them off-stage when they've overstayed their welcome.

Your Head is Faster than Your Hands

But there's an even deeper problem.

As it turns out, your brain is just too fast. (When was the last time you got *that* nice a compliment?!)

It's true.

Those little neurons are firing in your head at lightning speed. They're forming shapes. Ideas. Brilliance.

But your fingers are madly clicking away, trying desperately to keep up. Unfortunately, they're out here in the real world. Your fingers can't move at the speed of thought. So it's kinda like when you fall into a swimming pool. The resistance of the water is so strong, you can't just jump out again. You have to climb.

So imagine you're writing a page. You've got a clear idea of where you're going on that page. But as you get into it, suddenly those synapses start firing like crazy. Ideas spark ideas.

You get halfway through a sentence, and your brain shoots out in a new direction. Problem is, it's not the direction you intended to go on this page. But in the interest of speed (or "getting into the rhythm"), you follow that direction.

And then a couple paragraphs later, you realize you've gone astray. You're dangling precariously on the edge of this branch.

Not quite sure where you were going with this thread. Not quite sure how to tie all this back into your original idea.

You're lost. And frustrated. Again.

If this happens every time you try to write, it's no wonder you hate it so much! You equate "writing" with "impossible," because you can't harness your ideas.

And before you know it, you're in trouble. You're overwhelmed. It feels like you can't stay focused. And if you can't get through one page, how are you gonna complete a whole book? Why not just forget the whole thing?

Sound familiar?

The Idea Factory

It's not surprising that your brain is single-handedly responsible for most of your writing woes.

After all, your brain is where it all comes from. I call it the Idea Factory. And as an Idea Factory, your brain is pretty darned efficient.

Too efficient, sometimes.

Now, if you haven't been giving your brain enough stimulation (or the right *kind* of stimulation), you might think your Idea Factory is closed — out of business. You reach for an idea. You struggle to find it. You think and think until you have a headache. But, alas, you can't come up with an idea to save your life. That frustration is probably the biggest single killer of all failed writing careers. (They call it "Writer's Block.")

But when you stimulate your brain properly (which we'll get to in the Focus section), your Idea Factory kicks into overdrive. See, your mind is designed to come up with ideas. That's all it does. So if you let it, it will.

In fact, it'll come up with too many. It doesn't know when enough is enough, so it just keeps throwing ideas at you.

(If you don't have this problem yet, you're probably thinking it would be a *great* problem to have. But I assure you, it creates a whole new set of troubles.)

What happens is you get out there on a limb, and suddenly you have so many different possible directions to take it, you get paralyzed. Which idea is right? Which idea is best? Should I take my story *this* way or *that* way?

And you're back to square one.

Stopped. And struggling.

Here's what's really going on. Your idea exists in your mind, where all ideas are perfect. (Your Oscar-winner can confirm that for you.) It's perfect inside your mind because it's fuzzy around the edges. Your brain fills in the gaps. It says, "Don't worry about that missing part, something brilliant will go there."

But when you put it on the page, suddenly it's not as good. All those missing parts are just gaps. You read your work back, and it's nowhere near as good as it was in the Idea Factory. And the discrepancy kills you. You think you're terrible. And you run screaming into the other room.

You don't want to do it anymore. It never comes out right.

Two Different Worlds

It's just the difference between "Potential" and "Reality."

In your mind (when you think up this great idea), it's potentially brilliant. But look. *All* ideas are potentially brilliant. (In fact, when people come up to me and say they've got a great idea for a movie, I reply, "Excellent! How good is the screenplay?")

If you want the *reality* to be brilliant, you need to express your idea in the most effective way possible. And that's a judgment call. It's up to you to find the best words.

When you start typing, you're converting that potential into reality. And reality is never as glamorous as potential. Never.

You read your words back, and they bore you to tears.

Or they're confusing.

Or they're lame. Ineffective. Decidedly *not* compelling.

And you think you'll never get your idea out right. You get frustrated and angry and upset.

And you hate writing. And you vow never to do it again.

Understand this. You can — absolutely and positively — turn your idea into a reality as rich and accurate as what you had in your mind. Yes, you can. Yes. You can. Stop shaking your head.

You need to understand that this is a process. Yes, there are talented geniuses that fly through it without batting an eye. But for the rest of us, there's the process.

And that's what FAST is all about.

Taking your idea from potential to reality.

Judge, Jury and Executioner

It's important to understand how this Idea Factory works.

It never runs out of ideas. That's it's whole job.

Writer's Block is an imaginary thing. You only run into it when you stop stimulating your mind. See, the Idea Factory will churn out an endless number of ideas. I guarantee you it's limitless. The well will *never* go dry, if you stimulate it properly.

But there are some rules here. You've got to tap into the well. You've got to go with the flow.

You hate writing because you're expecting the Idea Factory to pump out *writing*. But it doesn't. It pumps out *ideas*. It's your job to harness those ideas and then shape them into your writing.

When you judge yourself too early, you break the production line of the Idea Factory.

Listen, one of the reasons speed writing is so effective is that it taps into the way your brain is designed to work. You're working *with* it, rather than *against* it the whole time.

Always remember: You can judge yourself later. If you stop doing it now, your writing speed will rocket forward.

And I'll tell you something. It was one of my biggest lessons.

I used to spend most of my writing time re-reading what I'd just written. Fixing, adjusting, tweaking. Notice that Tweak is the *last* step in the FAST System. That's because you just can't write if you don't let yourself go through the process.

When you do, that well produces more than you can handle.

I'll Get to It Later

No self-respecting book on writing would be complete without mentioning procrastination.

For some reason, we writers just love to do it. It's one of our favorite things.

When things haven't been going well, you look at that chair in front of the computer. And it terrifies you. You feel a little pain in your stomach.

But wait. What *is* that? Maybe you should go to the doctor! That's a sensible thing to do. So you go to the doctor.

And when you get back (it turned out you were fine), you

look at the chair again. But hey! The washing hasn't been done! You're not a slob, and you can't write with all this mess! So you get up and do it. In fact, while you're at it, it's been way too long since you did any dusting, too. Might as well get it all out of the way, so you can focus on your writing. And hey, while you're at it, you can't write on an empty stomach.

Oh, you'd write — no, you really would — but you're just never very productive when you're hungry—

Stop. Right now!

Procrastination will kill you.

And I don't mean that figuratively. I'm dead serious. Procrastination will *kill* you. It's laziness, pure and simple. You can justify it all you want. But if you want to finish your writing, you've got to sit your butt in that chair.

Whenever you're in the mood for procrastination, whip out this book. Crank up the Idea Factory, and jump into gear.

I promise you, it will vanish every time.

And so...

Know this, once and for all. Writing is *not* hard. It is not the painful challenge you think it is.

It's only painful and challenging when you're fighting it. When you're working against the process.

You won't hate writing when it's fun.

You'll tend to write *well* when you enjoy it.

And you'll only write brilliantly when you tap into it.

Writing well is a simple matter of tapping into the Idea Factory, and then harnessing what comes out of it, and shaping that into effective communication.

In the next chapter, we're going to take an in-depth overview of the FAST System. You'll see the exact process that allows you to do it, quickly and easily.

And then you'll love writing as much as the woman at the start of this chapter.

Just don't snicker at the ones who still struggle, okay?

You were there once, too, y'know.

3 **Meet the FAST System**

This chapter is the big one. In a few minutes, the way you think about writing is going to change forever.

So I should warn you. Do *not* drop this book and leap into your writing when you finish this chapter. It'll be tempting. You'll want to. But don't.

Please remember — this is only the final chapter of "The Setup" section. We're still just beginning! The idea might be clear, but we're *not* at the Payoff yet.

In fact, this chapter is only an overview. This book is structured in a very particular way to have a very specific effect.

It's designed to take you on a journey.

A journey *through* the FAST System. So that when you finish the book, you'll do more than just understand it. You'll *feel* it. And be able to *apply* it.

Now I've probably hyped this thing way too much. Maybe you're even skeptical at this point.

But it doesn't matter. Because you're about to see it for yourself. Last chapter, we looked at why you hate writing. This chapter, we'll explode every one of those reasons.

And because of the eye-opening you're about to have, it will be tempting to think you've got it all figured out. Just remember, the rest of the book goes into a lot more detail. And the picture won't be clear until we're done.

That's what good Setup and Payoff is all about.

There. I've said my piece. Let's meet the FAST System.

The FAST System Overview

The FAST System is a simple, step-by-step process for breaking any writing project down, and working through it systematically. The FAST System has four distinct phases:

Focus

In the Focus phase, you "Focus" your idea into a Plan. You'll start with a vague notion of what you want to write, and you'll turn that idea into a specific, detailed, step-by-step roadmap for your writing.

The objective of this phase is to create a writing plan for your project, complete with the specific details you'll write on each page of the project.

And don't worry. When you write FAST, Focusing your project will takes hours or days instead of months or years!

Apply

In the Apply phase, you "Apply" your Focus Plan. You'll fill all those blank pages with words as fast as you possibly can, using speed-writing techniques that get you in sync with your brain.

The objective of this phase is to fill pages. Nothing more. But since you've Focused your project, you'll be surprised to discover that your "rough draft" is much more solid than you expected.

This is where you'll get truly excited about your writing — when you discover the power of FAST.

Strengthen

In the Strengthen phase, you "Strengthen" what you've written. You'll use a very simple approach to see what you've got, what to do about it, and exactly how to make it stronger.

The objective of this phase is to make your writing match the ideas you're trying to express. By Focusing your idea, and Applying the plan, you know where you're going. Now, you push it there.

If you're moving systematically through this process, this is where your writing takes on a whole new life.

Tweak

In the Tweak phase, you "Tweak" your words to have the greatest possible impact. You'll finally get to judge your writing, and get meticulous with your presentation.

The objective of this phase is to make your work *read* fast! By waiting to tweak until the very last phase of your writing, you'll write faster than ever before. And now is your chance to grab and hold your reader.

You finish your entire project quickly and effectively, and your writing is stronger and better than ever.

* * *

And best of all, the FAST System fuels itself — the more you use it, the faster and easier it becomes. So let's get into it, shall we?

Why You Need a System

Writing without a system is like starting a three-thousand mile trek through the wilderness without a plan. It doesn't make good sense. You wouldn't just get to the edge of the city and start walking into the bush, would you?

Of course not. You'd never make it to the other side. There are just too many pitfalls along the way.

You need a roadmap.

The only problem is that when it comes to writing, every journey is different. No one can show you the road you're about to take, because no one's ever taken it before!

So pre-made roadmaps won't work. Formulas and methods are a bunch of hype. Instead, you need a system that helps you create your *own* roadmap.

And that's what the FAST System is all about.

I could tell you all about the Hollywood formulas and the classic three-act structures. They're great roadmaps — *if that's the road you're taking.* But the roadmap you'll create with FAST is original. Custom-tailored to you.

See, the FAST System isn't concerned with *only* the structure of your story, or *only* your words. It helps you through the whole process, from idea to completion. It's a way of looking at that hazardous terrain, and knowing exactly how to respond to the different kinds of troubles you're likely to encounter.

We'll break down your writing into manageable chunks — chunks you can handle easily and effectively. And then we'll move systematically through your work.

Look, confidence breeds success. When you successfully get through a phase of your writing, the struggle and the pain of it will slip away. You'll know exactly how to conquer it because you understand the system.

Three Definitions

When I talk about "writing FAST," the phrase really has three distinct definitions.

The first definition is the physical act of putting words onto the page as quickly as possible. Speed writing. I believe the faster you write, the better. For several reasons.

Firstly, when you write fast, you tap into that stream of ideas being continuously pumped out by the Idea Factory. Secondly, as you write faster, you approach the lightning speed of your mind. Thirdly, you get through the writing phase quicker, and reinforce positive neural pathways in your mind. And so on.

We'll get to more of that in the Apply section.

The second definition of "writing FAST" is the speed of the *read*. A well-written piece will always *read* fast. So if you're "writing FAST," you're actually being very kind to your reader. Writing only exists to be read, so the reader is the most important person to your writing. Right now, for example, you're more important than I am. I can put words on the page all day long. But it's all a waste of time if you don't understand them.

So when I talk about "writing FAST," don't just think of speed writing. That's only one part of the equation. The more important part is the speed of the *read*.

The third definition of "writing FAST" is *using* the FAST System to write your project. You're "writing FAST" when you go through this four-part process to get your projects written. The FAST System is this: Focus, Apply, Strengthen, Tweak.

You can speed write without using the FAST System. And you can create writing that *reads* fast without using the FAST System, too.

But either way, you're only using one third of the potential power of this book.

My goal is to get you doing all three. Speed writing *and* creating material that *reads* fast, *while* using the FAST System.

That's what I really mean by FAST.

Make sense?

Invent a Deadline

Now, technically, this isn't a requirement of the FAST System. But the whole idea of writing FAST implies a deadline. And I believe deadlines are the *only* way to get you to write.

When I started this book, I knew I wanted it to be written quickly. After all, what kind of credibility would I have if it took two years to write a book called "Writing FAST"?!

But, really, how long *should* it take? Who knows? It could

take two weeks or two years. Which will it be?

Believe it or not, that's a *choice*. You *decide* how long it takes. And it can just as easily take two weeks or two years. But you've gotta make that decision *deliberately*. And gear up for it.

Give yourself a hard and fast deadline. Even if it's arbitrary.

For example, when I decided to write this book, it was the first week of March, 2004. I decided to give myself a month (five weeks, actually) to write it. I wanted to finish by mid-April, so I could release the book by mid-May.

Why?

No real reason. I just wanted to finish it sooner than later. Then I could get back to FASTscreenplay, and then start building the Screenplay Factory.

But by setting a deadline, suddenly I've got a sharper focus. There's something constantly pulling at me. Rather than sitting in front of the TV, I'm here writing.

But I went a step further. I placed four ads in local writing newsletters *advertising the release date*. The ads came out in the April issues. So there was no backing away from the deadline. I had to do it. If I didn't want to, or didn't feel like it, too bad.

And I've gotta tell you, it's been pretty stressful. You might not want to do that just yet.

(Incidentally, I don't recommend that on your first book. I ran into production complications because I was new to the process, and had to delay the release by a whole month. It's not a good look.)

But give yourself a hard deadline. Not "next year." Make it closer than you think you can do. Force yourself to power through. Don't take the easy way out.

What's the Big Idea?

Now then.

The first stage of the FAST System is the F, for Focus. In the Focus phase, you'll turn your idea into a detailed Plan.

Inside that Idea Factory of yours, you've got a million thoughts floating around during every waking hour. (And every sleeping hour, too, even if you don't remember them.)

Remember how we said in the last couple chapters that all writing is communication?

Well, the first thing to understand is that all communication is *the transfer of ideas*. An idea pops into your head, and you want that idea to pop into someone *else's* head. That's what communication is. It's why we talk, shout, whisper, and write:

To share our ideas.

So the first thing we need to do before we start writing is determine the *idea* we're trying to communicate.

All writing — no matter how complex — has a single solitary idea at its very core. Take something as elaborate as a novel, or even a trilogy of thousand-page novels. At their very core lies a central idea. And everything you write needs to serve that central idea.

This applies to *all* writing.

Novels, screenplays, books, and other long-form writing may have larger, more complex, or more elaborate ideas at their core. They may also include dozens or even hundreds of smaller ideas tucked inside. But the central idea is the foundation.

Letters, web pages, emails, advertisements, pamphlets, short stories and other short-form writing will have simpler, smaller, narrower ideas at their core. And they'll nail the idea, as clearly and concisely as possible, and be done with it.

So it's important to *know your idea first*. Because everything else will stem from that.

For example, the idea of this book is encapsulated in the title: *Writing FAST: How to Write Anything with Lightning Speed*. That's the crux of the book. Its structure, its style, and its approach are all borne out of that. And everything in this book must serve that idea, and make it *clear*.

The First Priority

But clear to whom?

At the foundation of the Meisner Technique — the style of acting I was trained in (and subsequently taught) — was this basic idea:

"Put all your attention on the other actor."

It's an incredibly powerful idea. And it applies way beyond acting. Think about it.

Human nature is self-centered. That's not a bad thing, mind you. We're designed to be self-sufficient. To find our own food and shelter. So, naturally, we tend to look after ourselves.

But we end up *only* seeing ourselves. We stop noticing how other people we meet fit into the equation.

Yet, writing is communication. Transferring ideas. *What* you say (the words you use) is not important. What's important is that the reader understands! The other person is the most important thing here. So let's modify the quote to read:

"Put all your attention on the reader."

How can you express your idea so that *they* see it as clearly as you do? That's the key to writing.

Sure, different forms of writing have different objectives. When you write a letter, you want a different result than when you write a book. When you write a business report, you want a different result than when you write a screenplay.

Each type of writing will have a different *purpose*.

But each has a reader. And making that reader understand your idea is more important than any other thing.

In order to do this, you've got to *know the outcome*.

I used to balk at this idea. I always thought knowing the end before you started would stifle your creativity.

But as it turns out, that's not the case at all. In fact, if you don't know where you're going, you might not like where you end up! And if you get lost halfway through your writing, I can 100% guarantee it's because you didn't know where you were going when you started.

The Focus phase is where you determine that. It's where you'll flesh out your idea.

Break It Down Into Chunks

Once you've got your idea in place, you'll use the "chunking" technique. You'll break down your idea into manageable chunks, and lay it out on what I call the Power Grid. This is your roadmap.

The hardest part of writing is all those blank pages. That damn cursor blinking at you. At the bottom of the page, that little number says 1, and you have no idea what to do.

But chunking is the fine art of making it easy.

The first thing you'll do is estimate a total size of your work. For example, with this book, I estimated 200 pages. That's 192 numbered pages, and 8 preamble pages at the beginning.

But if I just started plowing into 192 pages of book, it would be incredibly easy to get lost. So, first thing I do is start chunking. I figure the best way to express the FAST System would be to break it into four sections: F. A. S. T. Makes sense, right?

But that's not quite enough. I need a Setup and a Payoff, so that'll make it *six* sections. And I'll throw in an introduction and an epilogue, to save my reader from hearing me yammer on and on about myself.

Then I start chunking it out. I estimate 6 pages for the Intro and Epilogue, which leaves 180 pages. Six equal sections would be 30 pages per section. I figure that'll divide nicely into three 10-page chapters apiece.

My chunking gives me a 30-page Setup section, 30 pages for each of the four-parts to the FAST System, and a 30-page Payoff section to show you how to apply it in the real world.

Suddenly, this enormous project is easily manageable. I don't have to write 192 pages. I only have to write 10.

And I just do it eighteen times.

Can you see how powerful the Chunking technique really is? You're making your own, custom-designed roadmap for your journey.

A formula created by *you*, especially for you.

The entire point of the Focus section is to turn your idea into a specific, step-by-step plan.

Master Talktation

The Focus phase of FAST could take as little as a day, or as much as a month or more. It's up to you, and it depends entirely on how much time you want to devote to it.

But once you're done, it's time for the second phase of the FAST System: A, for Apply.

Now that you've got your plan of attack, it's time to get your words on the page.

The Apply phase is where you write as fast as you possibly can. And that's a lot easier said than done, at first. You don't even know if you can *write*, let alone write *fast*!

That's why I've come up with a new approach to speed writing. I call it Talktation.

Talktation is similar to dictation, without the intermediary.

Dictation is where you speak into a recording device (a Dictaphone, usually, or a microphone on your computer), and then someone (could even be you) at a later time, listens back to the words, and transcribes them.

Dictation has one distinct advantage over typing or hand-writing. You can keep up with your speed of thought. See, we can talk much faster than we can type or hand-write, so when you speak, you're much more likely to keep up with the lightning speed of your mind.

Talktation is the act of training yourself to *type* at the speed of thought. Talking is easy. You don't judge yourself when you talk. So Talktation gets you to "talk" onto the page.

It's a conceptual technique. It's more of an idea than a physical technique. But you can physically practice to increase the speed of your writing. We'll take a closer look at it in Chapter 7.

The Apply phase is all about getting your words on the page *as fast as possible.* Don't analyze them. Don't think about them. Just get them on the page.

Look, no matter what you write, you'll *always* read it back later and find some way to fix it. So don't spend any more time than necessary getting your words on the page.

And *then* we'll see what we've got.

Twist It All Into Shape

After you've got the words on the page (which, at this point, you've done up to ten times as fast as you used to), you move onto the next phase of the process.

The third phase: S, for Strengthen.

You've been writing fast. You're getting your words on the page without *judging* them. Without thinking them to death. You've silenced the Movie Critic during the Apply phase.

Now it's time to let him out.

See, *while* you're writing, it's physically impossible to judge the quality of your work. You always try, even though it's impossible to do. And so you keep tripping yourself up.

But by applying Talktation, and getting your words onto the page with lightning speed, you've given yourself the freedom to judge your work when it's *ready* to be judged.

And that's now.

That's what the Strengthen phase is all about. Inspecting what you've got, intentionally looking for every flaw you can find, and then deciding what to do about it.

You'll use several techniques to decide what you've got and where to go with it, but the main one I've devised is called the Stack Test.

The Stack Test assumes your writing has a core idea you're trying to express (which you captured in the Focus phase). And in order for that idea to work, every single thing you write must build to it.

So you'll go through every paragraph you've written, and ask yourself if it belongs in the Stack. Is it building to the central idea? Or is it waste? Every section, every chapter, every paragraph, every sentence. Every last one of them must stack on top of each other to build to this point.

You'll have some decisions to make.

Maybe you'll decide whole sections must be re-designed. Or whole chapters need to be cut. Or sentences are useless.

Depending on what you've got, you'll either return to the Focus phase (where you'll Re-Focus, and start again), or you'll fill in holes in your knowledge (by Researching your details), or you'll rewrite, shift, cut and blend your work (a deliberate step I call the Edit grade), until your idea is clear.

Or you'll decide your work is building as it should, and it's time to Tweak this puppy.

Sharpen It Into a Fast Read

The final phase of the FAST System is T, for Tweak.

Most writers' biggest mistake is that they just can't resist tweaking *while* they're getting their words on the page. But tweaking is a Left-brain job, and getting words on the page is a Right-brain job. By giving each side of the brain its own time in the spotlight, we've freed you up to fly through it.

During the Tweak, we're not looking for structural changes. We're not asking ourselves if the idea is building. The Stack Test cleared all that for us. And you shouldn't even be *thinking* about the Tweak phase until you know for certain the work is solid.

When you get to the Tweak, it's about speed and impact.

Your attention is on the reader. You'll be reading your work as if you *were* the reader!

As a producer seeking screenplays, I was always astounded by how few writers seemed to care about the reader. They didn't bother to correct typos or adjust sentences to *control* the ride. You'd be shocked at some of the sloppy scripts I've seen.

You won't do that.

Tweaking is about grabbing the reader's eyeballs and pulling them down the page. At the speed *you* want them to go.

It's about fixing sentences, correcting grammar, and making sure your writing has the precise effect you want it to have.

And finishing it up in record time.

And so...

In a nutshell, that's the FAST System.

Different parts of FAST will be a revelation to different writers. Maybe the Focus section will be the eye-opener for you (it was for me!). It's so much more than just "outlining."

Or maybe the Apply section will be your true magic. Flying through your work (free to fix it later) is a glorious discovery.

Maybe the Strengthen section will be what kicks your project to life. The Stack Test and Strengthen Plan turn rewriting into a simple step-by-step process, after all.

Or it could be the Tweak section. There's something dazzling about controlling your reader's eyeballs.

But regardless of which section is your favorite, it's not any *one* section that makes the system such a breakthrough. What makes it a breakthrough is how they work *together* as a *whole*. Taken as a whole, this system has true, raw, genuine power.

Each stage makes the *other* stages easier. The Focus phase makes the Strengthen phase a breeze. The Apply phase can be *separated* from the Tweak phase. And so on.

Taken as a whole, you've now got a systematic approach for turning *any* idea into a compelling read.

Welcome to a new way of writing.

Pretty cool, huh?

[FOCUS]

Turn Your Idea Into a Plan

66 Organizing is what you do
before you do something,
so that when you do it,
it is not all mixed up. **99**

—A. A. Milne

4 Capture Your Idea

Ever since I can remember, I've been prone to leaping head-long into projects. An idea would spark in my mind, and my Oscar-winner would immediately hook his claws into it. I'd be whipped into a frenzy, and convinced I'd found my Holy Grail.

And I'd jump.

I'd race like a bat outta hell, furiously scrambling to finish the project in record time. Didn't matter what it was. I'd do it with movie projects, business projects, writing projects, everything.

But invariably, I'd get halfway through the project before I discovered its true scope. It would always happen the same way. I'd encounter a problem I wasn't expecting. Or a level of difficulty I couldn't see at the start. Or a dozen other complications.

And suddenly, the project becomes painful. The weight of the world falls on your shoulders. And it crushes you.

It ain't pretty.

It's dispiriting to work so hard on a project and feel nothing but a sense of *obligation*. Projects should carry a sense of *excitement* and *anticipation*. Not despair!

That's why this section of the book holds the most meaning and importance for me, personally. This was my revelation.

Listen, I'd heard it all before. I knew all about "outlining" and "mapping" and "blueprinting" and "planning" your work. I'd heard it all from all the best sources. In a dozen different ways. But I continued to run the other way.

I didn't want to "stifle my creativity." Writing is magic, I said, and you just have to tap into it. Besides, I don't want to waste all that *time* planning my writing. (Recognize that?)

But here's the jaw-dropper.

I discovered a secret.

When you take the time to Focus your idea *first*, you actually allow yourself to write *faster*. You tap into that magic more *directly*. And you don't get lost halfway through.

It's ten times more valuable than we ever imagined.

The Objective of this Phase

F is for Focus.

The Focus phase is about one thing: Turning Your Idea into a Plan. And "Focus" is the perfect word for it. Because it's all about *focusing* your intentions.

And here's the best part. The more effort you put into this phase, the easier the next phases become. Why? Because each builds on the one before. And it all starts with an idea.

The Focus phase has three distinct steps.

Step One: Capture your idea.

Before you start, you've either got a hundred ideas swirling inside your brain, or you've got *none*. Either way, we need to capture the exact idea you're going to communicate. We don't want it to get muddy, or slip through your fingers mid-stream.

Step Two: Make your idea specific.

Once you've got the idea, it could take any one of a million different shapes. Movies are a great example of that. How many times do we see the same basic idea told in very different ways? (Remember the animated movies *Antz* and *A Bug's Life*? Virtually identical ideas told in different ways.)

Step Three: Turn that idea into a specific plan that will guide you as you write.

This one is the clincher. Once you've nailed your idea, you'll stretch it out over your canvas like form-fitting elastic. You'll give yourself a step-by-step guide to finishing. Finishing *your* way.

And the more *detail* you include in your plan, the better. It's a paradox. The more you nail it down, the more flexibility you have. (And, oh man, was that a *massive* revelation for me.)

If you want to write *fast*, the Focus phase is the secret!

You'll grab your ideas (or *create* them if you don't have any), and design a roadmap. That's what this phase is all about.

Don't start writing — not even a single word! — until you've finished this phase. It'll save you a lot of unnecessary work. And you'll *really* tap into the magic of writing.

The Elusive Idea

Ideas are incredibly slippery little beasts. They're almost impossible to grab. They pop into your head without warning.

But as you reach for one, it slides out from between your arms. You wait for it to come back. But you sit there for days or weeks racking your brain, and it never returns.

I know. We've all been there.

When you "capture" an idea, you're able to hold onto it. You don't forget it. You don't lose it. And it doesn't keep disappearing because a "better idea" takes its place.

The rest of this chapter is about capturing your idea.

If you struggle, you're generally in one of two groups.

The first group has *no* ideas. None. At all. You know you want to write a novel or a movie or whatever. But you have no idea what to write *about*. You need to capture *something*.

The second group has too *many* ideas. They're gushing out of you like you're a leaky tap. You can't decide which way to go. And you're just as stuck as if you had no ideas in the first place. You need to capture the *right* thing.

In both cases, you're looking for your central idea.

And there's only one way to capture it.

One Single Sentence

Write it down in one single sentence.

That's it. I'm serious. Not a one-page overview. Not a detailed outline. Not a crisp, clear paragraph. One single sentence. And nothing more.

That's your central idea.

And simple is better. *Always*. It's the core of your project.

If you don't do this (like when you race in without a plan), your ideas get muddled, or they vanish into thin air.

And, yes, I know. You're writing a novel or a movie or other long-form project, and you can't possibly whittle the whole concept down to one single sentence.

Oh, but you can. And you must.

Take an example I use in my screenwriting workshops: the movie *The Shawshank Redemption*. Here's a quote from the opening page of that script, which is also a line from the movie:

"Hope is a good thing, maybe the best of things, and no good thing ever dies..."

That's the central idea of that movie. And when you know your central idea, you can hold everything else up against it.

You can hold up every idea, every scene, every page, every word you write. And ask, "Does this build the idea — or not?"

Keep it simple. The more convoluted your central idea, the more confusing or disjointed for the reader. It's too easy to lose them. Your reader wonders what the heck you're trying to get at.

And *you* forget the whole purpose of your project.

With a clear central idea, you'll stay on target.

Get excited about it

Now, in order to capture an idea, it helps if you actually *like* the idea (or are fascinated by it, at least).

But even if you're forced to write on assignment — and you absolutely *hate* the idea — try to find an angle to connect with.

The most effective writing is captivating. You know the kind. Where you can just tell — you can almost *feel* — the writer really *loves* what he's writing about.

Think about the last time you were in a conversation with a friend, and you got excited. Maybe you were telling a story, or anticipating something, or reliving a great moment you shared.

Did you stand there like two cardboard statues? Of course not! You bounced around, waving your arms — laughing — the pitch of your voice going all over the place.

Why? Because you were excited! You had a passion for the idea, and you were *enjoying* sharing it with your friend.

Good writing works exactly the same way.

Take *my* writing, for example. Is there a life in it? (Jeez, now that I mention it, I sure hope so!) I can't stay excited the whole time — we'd both get worn out!

But you can still sense it, can't you? That I'm excited about this FAST System?

Well, you can also sense when I get *bored*. Know how? It's when *you* get bored, too!

See, how you feel about your topic comes across to the reader. Every time. So start on the right foot.

Pick topics and ideas that are meaningful to you. Ideas you enjoy. And then get excited about them! The stronger your connection to it, the more powerful your writing will become.

Don't just snatch up any old idea (or worse — the first one that comes to mind)! Take some time to consider how you feel about it. C'mon, life is short! You should do what you *want* to do. You should write what you *want* to write.

You'll write *better*, too. Even a homework assignment (I used to hate those) can be fun — if you infuse *yourself* into it. Bring your own passion to the assignment, and you'll fly through it.

I don't think they taught that in school. Pity.

Use Your Fear to Find It

If you already know your "one single sentence" — if you can already crystallize it — don't complicate it. Sometimes it's just that simple. Take it and run with it.

But sometimes it's really *not* that simple. You feel like you couldn't capture your idea if your life depended on it.

When you really struggle — when it gets painful — you've got to look in a different place entirely. Because your idea is hiding.

It's hiding behind your *fear*.

Fear can be a valuable emotion. But we need to understand something about fear. It's a physiological electro-chemical process in your brain. It's there to make sure you survive life-threatening situations.

And I gotta tell ya something.

Nothing about writing is life-threatening. *Nothing*.

Your computer is never going to attack you. I promise. Well, maybe some day, as part of a virtual reality game or something. But even then, it won't happen while you're writing.

And even if your writing is the worst, most atrocious string of words ever to grace the page (which would be interesting in itself), you're still not going to *die* from it.

And even if everyone who reads it *hates* it, you'll still be breathing. So you'll pick yourself up, and try again. No worries.

But notice the fear. When you're afraid of something, it's a sign. It's the biggest clue your brain will ever give you. It's telling you exactly what you need to do. Your brain is saying, "I'm terrified, because if you pursue this idea, I'll have to live up to it."

"Do what you fear most." Let that be your personal mantra. We only fear what we don't know or understand. So when you tackle a fear head-on, you'll conquer it every time.

Same with your ideas. Actively *follow* the fear. Pursue it. If you're afraid of something, or you resist it, chances are, the idea you're trying to capture is hiding underneath.

Fear is a diversionary tactic your brain uses to stay lazy.

Call its bluff.

Nail the Real Idea

Your brain's got another trick up its sleeve, too.

It holds out on you.

Here's what it doesn't want you to know: The best ideas can only be reached by going *through* a series of *lame* ideas.

See, your brain throws out mediocre ideas first, to see if you're paying attention. You ask for ideas, and, okay, it chucks out a couple nuggets.

But it's only testing you.

If you take those first nuggets and let that Oscar-winner go wild, the brain sits back and says, "Too easy." It knows you'll jump at anything, so it doesn't have to work very hard.

Only one problem. It then *doesn't* work very hard. You've trained it, just like you'd train a puppy. Except you did it backwards. You trained your brain to *make* a mess on the rug.

Don't settle for the first idea you come up with.

The first idea is almost always your brain's lazy way of avoiding any real effort. It's understandable. We all do it. No animal on Earth expends more energy than it has to. And that's why people are lazy. It's natural. It's innate.

But it kills your writing.

Always dig deeper. Find the *real* idea underneath the first few nuggets. Unless you're completely 100% certain you've nailed the best possible approach to whatever it is you're writing, you can't stop there. You've got to look beyond.

You've got to see where those nuggets lead.

Let Ideas Spark Ideas

The key is to let go. Don't try to steer it.

This mind of yours is really an amazing tool. I'm not sure if we really appreciate the power of it.

I keep calling it an Idea Factory, which might conjure up images of a cold, grey, mechanical environment, with lots of levers and conveyor belts and stuff.

But I don't see it like that. I picture the brain with that image they use on science documentaries. You know the one. All those nerve endings branching out like a tree that won't quit. With the little electrical pulses that go pumping through the mesh to indicate a thought.

That's the Factory. It's electric. It's vibrant. It buzzes with energy. Ideas spark each other at lightning speed. And they gather momentum — if you let them. This idea sparks the next idea, which sparks the one after it.

Imagine all that going on in your brain right now. It's happening *right now!* C'mon, at least take a moment to think about how cool that is.

And when you *do* think about it, I want you to realize it's where your ideas come from. Those bolts of electricity.

Each idea — each lightning bolt — that pops into your head, can spark a thousand more. But you're in control of the Factory, so you've got to give it permission.

If you're struggling, start a chain reaction. Let one idea spark the next, which sparks the next. See where *it* takes *you*.

I guarantee you one thing. If you truly let go, you'll arrive at the greatest and most compelling ideas you've ever come up with. You will genuinely astound yourself.

But it only works if you let go.

The Great Storm

If we use this lightning speed analogy, and think of the electrical pulses in our brains as lightning bolts, it gives the word "brainstorm" a much more dynamic meaning, dontcha think?

Personally, I imagine a wicked electrical storm, throwing bolts of ideas out in every direction. It's one vibrant, almost uncontrollable rush of energy and madness, all at the same time. It's dark and mysterious, yet incredibly powerful and consuming.

Oddly enough, that's exactly what it's *supposed* to be.

When you think of a brainstorming session, what do you imagine? A bunch of businessmen sitting around a boardroom table, throwing ideas onto a whiteboard?

No way! It's much more dynamic than that.

And it's a tool *you* can use to find and capture exactly the right idea.

Brainstorming is simple. You think up as many ideas as you possibly can. You let your mind roam free. You don't judge anything. The weirdest, craziest, most off-the-wall ideas that pop into your head get put down on paper, too.

In fact, that's the entire secret to brainstorming. Don't judge *anything*. Let ideas spark ideas. Write down *everything*. If I say the word "car", you immediately picture a car in your head, right? Good. Now brainstorm.

What kind of car is it? It's probably either the one you drive, or the one you *want* to drive. Great. Now what do those images spark? Write a list of *everything* that pops into your head.

What about car-related items? Things like keys, and wheels, and tires, and windshields, and doors and windows. Or things that aren't *on* the car, but are car-related. Things like insurance, fuel, accidents, registration, squeaks, rattles and...

And your mind is off and running.

For your writing project, brainstorm the *central idea* of the piece. It could be a theme, a moral, a concept, or anything. But it's the whole idea you're trying to put in the reader's head.

The key to brainstorming is to avoid judgment. You can judge it later. When you start, just get ideas on the page. You want to capture one, right? Well, you just might need to let a few sparks go off before you can get there.

Just remember to write them down.

When you do, you can pluck the idea that works.

This quick little car example gave me an analogy:

Ideas are like hit-and-run drivers. They have a funny way of appearing from out of nowhere, broadsiding you, and then disappearing, and never coming back.

Capture them now, or they'll be gone forever.

Capture Your Idea in 5 Easy Steps

So let's make a quick list of steps for capturing your idea. Do this list in this order. And really *do* it.

1. <u>See what you've got</u>.
   You may already have your idea. If you do, don't complicate it. Skip to #5. But if it's not clear, crisp, original, compelling and interesting to you (honestly), then:

2. <u>Look beyond the obvious</u>.
   Ask yourself what you're really trying to say. Is this thought leading somewhere else? Somewhere you're hesitant to go? Think about it. Then:

3. <u>Brainstorm a new list of ideas</u>.
   Don't judge or think or steer. Create an enormous list of every possible approach to your idea. Take as much time as you need! Let yourself go. Scan the list, and look for the one that jumps out at you. Then:

4. <u>Take it to its conclusion</u>.
   Don't settle for the first nuggets your brain gives you. Ask yourself what *about* this idea is compelling. Follow that train. Let the idea spark ideas, and lead you to the exact idea you want to express. You'll know it in your bones when you hit it. And then:

5. <u>Write it down in one single sentence</u>.
   As clear and sharp as possible. Not a giant extended sentence that goes forever. One short, brief sentence that represents the essence of the idea you're trying to express.

This whole process could take days, or weeks, or more! In fact, right now, your brain is working on ideas you've put into motion years ago. The Idea Factory never closes.

Or, it could take less than a minute. Sometimes you just know. Don't over-complicate it. Remember, the point is simple. Give yourself a foundation upon which to build.

When you've got it, you've got it. When you don't, come back to this list, and *play*. Let the Factory do the work.

And so...

One of the major lessons here, which has hopefully been woven subtly throughout this chapter, is that *you must do this*. One way or another, you will never write anything until you've got an idea you're trying to express. So you might as well spend a little extra time nailing it down.

I was a fool. I rushed it. Don't be a fool, too. Even if you don't think you need this step, be aware. You're doing it whether you realize it or not.

The only difference is whether you're clear about your idea, or if it's jumbled up with a million other ideas in your mind.

When I raced through this chapter the first time, I had a plan for what I was writing (which I'll explain in more detail in Chapter 6). But I hadn't nailed down my idea.

I was spinning my wheels, and getting nowhere. I spent hours of frustration figuring out which way to go.

When I realized that, I stopped. I took fifteen minutes (that's all it took!) to nail the idea of this chapter. I stripped away all the nonsense — all the crap that was getting us nowhere — and asked myself, "What am I really trying to say, here?"

My one-sentence answer was "How does a writer capture his idea?" Man. Seriously. How simple is that?

It focused me like a laser on the task at hand. I wrote the chapter in less than three hours.

Sometimes it's simple. Sometimes it takes a little more work.

But it's the most *leveraged* work you can do.

Because when you capture your idea, you're ready to build.

5

Make Your
Idea Specific

In the last chapter, you captured your idea. You saw it. You felt it. You tasted it. You knew for certain — without a shadow of doubt — the *precise* idea you're going to write about.

Right?

You've got it nailed, right?

You do, don't you? Don't... you?

Wait. What do you mean, "not quite"? You mean you're still not sure? You mean the whole "100% certain" thing didn't quite happen for you?

Well, listen. Don't worry. It's really not a problem.

Hang on. Am I changing my tune?

Absolutely not. The more clearly you see your idea, the easier your writing will be. Only when it's crystal clear in your mind can you effectively express it.

But there's something that's even *more* important than nailing your idea. It might even be the most important thing of all:

Not getting stuck.

Don't let yourself get stuck on *any* phase of writing. Keep moving forward. There's no law that says you have to capture your idea before you start. I think it helps. I've seen it speed everything up. But if it's slowing you down, *come back to it*.

I don't mean you can't think, or ponder, or weigh up different choices. I don't even mean you shouldn't *struggle* with it. Sometimes the struggle is *good* — your brain is figuring out the optimal solution. Struggle can lead to dramatic results.

But what you can't do — what you must *never* do — is stop moving forward. The FAST System is here to help you build momentum. Don't let it get you stuck. Remember to be flexible. It's a guide. An *approach*. Not a set of rules.

Do a phase, move on. Anything you write now probably *will* be changed later anyway. So don't sweat it. Maybe you need to "find" your idea by working *through* it.

Just be sure that when you finally *do* nail your idea, you write it in one sentence. You'll need that for the Strengthen phase.

Now then.

Ready or not, it's time to make your idea specific.

How to Make an Idea Specific

First, let's define "specific."

Remember, you're trying to get your idea into the reader's head. That's the most important thing. But because there are so many ways to express an idea, you've got to choose one.

Your idea itself is amorphous. You can't touch it or hold it or feel it. You need to give it *shape*. You'll need to find some way to allow your reader to hold it. A way to make it stick.

Take the *Shawshank Redemption* example. "Hope is a good thing, maybe the best of things, and no good thing ever dies..."

It's a very powerful idea. It's worth sharing. It's worth communicating. But does it *mean* anything to you? Does it hit you in the gut? Probably not.

It's just words.

To communicate the idea — to really get the reader to understand it, we need to turn that *idea* into something *tangible*.

How does *Shawshank* make that idea tangible?

By telling the story of a man sentenced to life in prison — a man who refuses to let the horrors of prison crush his spirit. And by *contrasting* his attitude with that of his inmate friend — a man who has given up hope of a life outside the prison's walls.

They've *shown* the idea. They've given "hope" a face. And a context. They've *demonstrated* that "hope is a good thing..."

By turning it into a tangible story — a story we can see and grasp — the idea springs to life. The *idea* can be understood in the minds of the readers.

Could the same idea ("Hope is a good thing...") take a different shape? Absolutely! That idea could be expressed a thousand different ways.

By giving the idea this *specific* shape, the idea has this *specific* effect. If you present it another way, it'll have a different effect.

All writing must serve its central idea.

The writing itself is the *shape* of that idea.

To make your idea "specific," then, you simply decide how you want your idea to be demonstrated.

The Best Demonstration

Different kinds of writing have different requirements.

Your job is to find the most effective way to say it. Not only for the *idea* you're expressing, but also for the type of writing you're targeting.

For example, if you're writing a screenplay, the tangible *shape* of your idea is a "story." In fact, when you're writing fiction of any kind, you're expressing your idea *through* story.

A screenplay requires a *visual* story. A story told through external action and dialogue.

On the other hand, a novel takes us *inside* the characters' minds. It might use smells and the sense of touch in a way a screenplay never could. You might carefully weave dozens of characters through hundreds of story threads. There are a million different possibilities.

But to create a story of any kind, think of it this way. You have an idea. Your reader doesn't understand it. You need to give her an example. That *example* is your story. The story is the idea personified.

Non-fiction's *shape* is different. But the same principles apply.

If you're writing a book like this one, it won't be a story. Instead, it might be a *system*, or a *metaphor*, or a *hook* (or anything else you can come up with).

For example, my *idea* for this book (in one single sentence) is "How to write anything with lightning speed." That's the idea. But how do I *express* that idea? I've chosen to demonstrate each stage of the FAST System. When you (the reader) see the whole *process*, I believe my *idea* will be clear to you. (And if it's not, good gawd, let me know immediately so I can revise this thing!)

Every form of writing is different.

A magazine article might need a hook or a gimmick. A news story might find an "angle." An ad may need to present an over-all benefit. A letter might use an event or a "lesson." A business plan might try a "vision." A review might explore an analogy.

Use your imagination. Be original. *How* you demonstrate your idea is the very essence of your writing. It's you. It's your voice. It's the nature of your communication.

And the principle is always the same.

Demonstrate the idea. Make it tangible. Give the reader a way to understand.

Jump In

The first thing to do, is just go for it.

Forget the fear of being "wrong." There's no right or wrong, and you'll make plenty of changes to this stuff as you go. Remember, ideas spark ideas. You'll have *better* ideas *later*. For now, don't worry about "getting it right." Just jump in.

Let's imagine *Shawshank* didn't exist, and we were creating it. It probably didn't happen this way, but I want to show you the process for making your idea specific.

You start with the idea ("Hope is a good thing, maybe the best of things, and no good thing ever dies..."), and you want to make it tangible. You want to turn it into a movie.

So, let's see. You start out by thinking about hope itself. What is it? It's that feeling of anticipation. It's when you *want* something, and believe it's likely to happen. Maybe we could use contrast. We could show a *hopeless* situation.

So what's a hopeless situation? How about prison? How about showing a man (Andy) facing life in prison for a crime he claims he didn't commit. He maintains *hope* that he'll be released, and his name will be cleared.

Not a bad start. We'll jot that down.

So where do we go from here?

Now, let's build upon it. "Hope is a good thing..." In order to make that argument, we need to show the opposing viewpoint. We could have a character who *doesn't* agree. How about a sec-ond character (Red) — an inmate who has no hope at all? He's been rejected for parole three times, and figures he'll die in this prison. In fact, he believes hope is *dangerous* in a place like this.

Okay. Jot that down. That gives us a way to show different sides to this idea. But it's not going to make the audience *feel* it yet. The idea still isn't really tangible enough.

What if we give Andy disappointment after disappointment after disappointment? Span the story across twenty years. Push him to despair. And because of the friendship they've formed, Red's concern for his friend *gives* him hope. Let Red *discover* hope through his friendship with Andy.

And when he does, the idea becomes clear to the audience. It'll hit them in gut. And they'll *feel* it.

Make sense?

This is how you make your idea specific. You simply give it a specific shape. A shape that *demonstrates* the idea.

Create a Preview

I really hope I haven't made this too confusing.

Sometimes I read back what I've written, and it makes sense to *me*, but I wonder if it's gonna make sense to *you*. As a writer, you'll have that same worry — a lot. (That's why I mentioned it.)

Let me simplify all this.

This chapter is about turning your idea into a story (or, if you're writing non-fiction, finding a tangible shape).

That's it.

It's no more complicated than that.

In order to write your story (or your book, or article or thesis or whatever), you'll create a Focus Plan.

But in order to *do* it, we need to be clear on where we're trying to go. We need a way to stay on track.

So we'll start with what I call a Preview.

A Preview is the overview of *how you're going to present your idea*. If we're talking about screenplays, I might call it a "pitch" or a "synopsis." It's the whole story in one paragraph or one page. But it doesn't have to be that formal, so I'm calling it a Preview, instead.

Basically, you sketch out your story, like we just did with *Shawshank*. Not just in your mind, but physically on paper. If you're writing a book, maybe you'll sketch out the main points of each phase, and how you're going to present the information. Or the hook, or the steps of the metaphor you're using.

By putting it on paper, you give yourself something to work with. You capture the idea, and start molding it.

Personally, I like to use blank sheets of paper, and physically sketch it out. Mine looks like the doodling of a three year-old.

It's going to start like *this* (I'll draw a line across a page going upwards) and then come together like *that* (I'll make a big circle). And then each of the points will be here, here, and here (and I'll draw squiggly lines where the points will go). I'll plop down the story points, or maybe list images I'm trying get across, in the order I think they'll go.

The shape it takes is entirely up to you.

The point is to create a Preview — a rough sketch of the end product. An overview of the story, the book, the proposal, the biography, whatever. It's the *way* you're expressing your idea.

Setup and Payoff

The concept of Setup and Payoff can give your project a shape more quickly than just about anything else I can think of. I believe everything you write will fall into one of these two categories. Just by being aware of it, your ideas will take shape almost without any effort at all.

A setup needs a payoff. And a payoff doesn't pay anything off without a setup.

Take *this* sentence for example. Was it setup or payoff?

Answer: It was setup. *This* sentence is the payoff!

The setup "sets up" the idea. It builds the context. It creates the anticipation of "more-to-come." When she reads the setup, your reader expects something more.

The payoff answers it. It closes the gap. It completes the idea in the mind of the reader.

Remember that caveman analogy in the first chapter? Remember how I told you I'd give you the answer later? Well, that was a setup. It opened the thought, and created an incomplete idea. If we want to *close* that idea, we've got to pay if off.

What did you think the payoff to that story was? Did you think it was when the image of the mammoth filled their minds? That was a payoff, yes. But a larger payoff was the line "And written communication was born." It pays off the whole story.

Fact is, they were *both* payoff lines. But that story has an even *bigger* payoff. It's the line (on page 12) "You saw the mammoth." Because with that line, I didn't just payoff the story, I made the *story itself* payoff.

Make sense? Good. Because the previous two paragraphs were the payoff for the "I'll tell you later" setup on page 13.

See how it works?

Of course you do. Because that was the payoff for *this* segment. (Wow, what a head-trip.)

Every payoff should be a new revelation. But it only works when you've set it up effectively.

When you're creating the Preview for your idea, break it down into setup and payoff. The payoff is the kicker. It's where your reader grasps the *central idea* you're going for, even if you never say the idea directly.

The Reader's Journey

Think of your writing as a journey for the reader.

When I sat down to organize this book, I knew I wanted to take you through the FAST System. I knew I wanted to give you a section for each of the phases. One for Focus, one for Apply, one for Strengthen, and one for Tweak.

But, really, what's the best way to present that?

I could've been intellectual, and shown you all the underlying scientific motivations for every phase. I could've bored you silly. (If you think it's *already* boring, you should see what I've cut!)

Or I could've been extremely sparse. I could've presented a whole book of checklists and point-by-point instructions. Do this first. Then do this. Then this. Then this. But I believe there's way too much variety in writing. It's too personal. What you write needs to come from *you*. No cookie-cutter approach is going to be effective.

So I've opted for a very specific alternative. In each chapter, I'm trying to take you *through* the idea of the chapter. I want you to feel like you're *inside* the idea. But your journey should be practical, too. So I summarize with "5 easy steps" so you can put the idea into motion.

I've written it this way because I believe it'll help you *feel* it. And if you *feel* it, I think you'll be able to *do* it.

Does it work? I dunno. Only *you* can be the judge.

But as the writer, you've got to take your best guess. Focus on the reader's journey. Design the ride you think will get your idea across most effectively.

Test it Out

Once you've got your idea fleshed out, it's time to test it. A few simple tests make all the difference in the world.

One test is whether or not your Preview makes sense. Are you telling a story? Make sure it's interesting, has a point, and takes the reader on a ride. Look for holes and logic flaws.

Are you writing non-fiction? Same thing. Make sure your idea is clear and tangible. Will your approach really put your idea inside your reader's mind? Think about it. Hunt for missing elements. It's much easier to fix it now than after you've got it all written out.

Another test is whether or not your Preview is actually *effective*. If you can't tell, and you don't have a very good sense of these things, don't risk it. Ask someone. Get some feedback. Show your Preview to someone who can be objective. Don't ask them whether it's "good" or not; ask them whether the idea is *clear*. And don't avoid this because you're afraid of rejection. It's easier to change course *now* than after you've been working on it for months!

And one last test of your Preview is whether or not you can *expand* it. This happens all the time. You get a great idea, you build your Preview, and then when we get to the next step, you have no idea where to go. It's crucial for long-form writing. Make sure your idea is full and rich enough for all those pages!

Listen, the point is this.

Don't race into it. If you're anything like me, you want to get your writing over and done with. It's a pain in the butt, and you'd rather just finish it as quickly as possible and move on.

But if you race into it, you're just making it harder on yourself. Test your idea first and make sure you're running in on solid ground. Think carefully about the best way to hit this idea.

Because once we get through the next chapter, the real fun begins.

Make Your Idea Specific in 5 Easy Steps

Once you've got your idea, it's time to give it shape, and form. Here are five easy steps to get there.

1. <u>Consider your idea</u>.
   Put your idea in your mind. Mull it over. Think about the different shapes it could take. Ask yourself what it means to you. Let your gut take over. Then:

2. <u>Make it tangible</u>.
   Remember, your reader needs to grasp your idea. Give them something to hold. Create an *example* of that idea. Give it a specific *shape*. Play with different concepts and approaches, and then:

3. <u>Test your approach</u>.
   Put yourself in your reader's shoes, and vigorously challenge your concept. Look for holes or weaknesses, or anything that's confusing. If you can't be objective, get feedback. And once you're happy with it, then:

4. <u>Flesh it out</u>.
   Make it specific. Create an overall chain of thought. Let it build. For fiction, lay down some major turning points. For non-fiction, sketch out your *approach* to the material. Then:

5. <u>Create your Preview</u>.
   It ain't real until you put it on the page. So do it. It could be one paragraph, or a full page. It could be a chart, a map, or a drawing. Whatever works for you. As long as you can see it, touch it, and hold it. This Preview is going to help you create your Focus Plan in the next section.

Like everything else in this book, these steps could take you as little as two minutes, or as much as a few weeks. It all depends on what you want to do. There's no right or wrong.

If you want my advice, do it quickly. Don't over-think it. Go with your instinct. Make it solid, but remember — don't let yourself get stuck! You can *always* change it later.

And so...

The first two chapters of the Focus section have been about figuring out exactly what your idea is, and deciding on the best way to express it.

In the next chapter, we're going to take that idea, and turn it into a detailed, step-by-step approach to your writing. You're going to create your own, one-of-a-kind roadmap.

Your own personal formula, to help you blast through it.

The clearer your idea, the easier it will be to create your Focus Plan. So don't skimp on these first two chapters just because the meat of this phase is in the next one.

Take the time to nail your idea.

I've made this mistake myself a thousand times. And I've even made it repeatedly while writing this book! And every time I make the mistake of rushing into the next phase, it slows me down and makes the work ten times harder than it needs to be.

If you really want to write ten times faster, capture your idea and make it specific *first*. It has a trickle-down effect.

A little effort here makes a world of difference later.

And once you've got your idea, and know (or think you know) how you're going to present it, get ready for the ride of your life.

6 Attach Your Lightning Rod

Here comes the raw power of the FAST System.

I hope you're holding onto your seat, because this is where it gets interesting. This is where we ignite the engine, and launch your writing to a whole new level.

You've got a clear picture of your idea — and you've got your one single sentence to prove it.

You know the shape it's going to take. You've got the Preview of your story, the basic mechanics of your metaphor, or your system, or your approach. You might even have a sketch, or a synopsis, or an outline sitting at the ready.

This chapter is where we convert those things into your own personal lightning rod. We'll harness the power of your mind and the power of your ideas.

Now if you *don't* have those things, it's alright. You can still power forward and work through your idea.

But I hope you're not just reading this book to get the "gist" of it. I hope you're not thinking, *Once I've got it figured out, I'll come back and actually apply it.*

Because I've got to warn you. You won't get the full power out of this until you physically *apply* it. Here's why.

You read something. Your brain engages intellectually with it. You think to yourself, *Okay, yeah, I can see that.*

But when you *apply* it, you *feel* it. You *experience* it. And an experience involves multiple senses at the same time. An *experience* involves your eyes, ears, brain, nerve endings, sense of touch

— it even involves your emotional *response* to the whole experience. It's three-dimensional.

It'll stay with you longer. A *lot* longer. Because it's not just your *brain* remembering it. Your nerves remember it, too. Your emotions remember it. Your fingertips remember it.

If all you do is *read* this stuff, you miss that whole layer of understanding. So I urge you to *apply* it.

See for yourself just how powerful it really is.

The Lightning Rod

A lightning rod is a large metal pole that's attached to the top of a building to attract stray bolts of lightning, and protect the structure itself from damage.

The lightning rod harnesses the lightning.

Well, I want to you to imagine your project. Imagine it laying flat across the floor. And above you, your brain is storming. Your thoughts are lightning bolts, shooting out in every direction.

Now, imagine if you could attach a lightning rod to your work, and harness that power. Suppose you could control it. Steer it. Put that voltage exactly where you want it.

And every time a bolt of lightning shot out from your mind, your lightning rod would capture it, funnel it, and direct it to the exact spot and moment in your writing where you need it most.

Sound like something you could use?

Good. Because that's precisely what we're going to do.

We're going to funnel the power of your mind directly into your work. We'll attach this lightning rod to your idea, or, more specifically, to the *shape* of your idea. We'll anchor it down in key positions, so that each idea, each bolt of lightning, will shoot you forward through your work.

It takes the effort, the pain, and the struggle, right out of the equation. Those troubles only arise when you don't know where to go. With your lightning rod, you'll know exactly.

Create a Power Grid

To *use* this lightning rod, we have to attach it to the right spots, or it won't work. Each bolt of lightning — each idea — can *fuel* your work, or it can *fry* it. And you don't want to fry it.

So, instead, you'll plug that rod into the Power Grid.

Have you ever seen a picture of Los Angeles at night? The entire L.A. basin is laid out like a grid. Thousands of little square blocks sitting in orderly rows.

At night, from an observatory overlooking the city, you can see the street lights sparkle in perfectly symmetrical lines that go all the way to the horizon. It's quite beautiful.

Well, imagine your writing spread out across that grid. It doesn't matter if it's a thousand-page novel, or a one-page letter. See it there on the ground. Picture each page spread end-to-end, every page touching the edge of the page next to it.

The first page of your writing is at your feet. And your pages stretch as far as the eye can see. The last page is at the horizon.

And hovering *over* your pages is the Power Grid. Instead of city streets, those sparkling lines are electric currents. Energy pumps through them. You can see the pulse of the current.

Now imagine that *each* square of the Grid hovers over one *page* of your writing. Can you see it? Energy — your idea — flows through the Grid, buzzing around the edges of every page.

When you attach your lightning rod to this grid, you can *harness* those stray bolts of lightning, and pump them straight into the power line. You'll pump your ideas right *into* your writing. And when you do, each bolt of lightning goes exactly where you need it.

That's what this final step in the Focus stage is about.

It's about "focusing" your idea onto that grid.

And we do it by creating a Plan.

Broad Strokes to Micro Strokes

First, you'll pull out the Preview you created in the last chapter. You'll look at your idea's shape. Then you'll stretch that shape out across the grid.

And then you'll zoom in to each block of the grid, and plan what goes there.

In simpler terms (and without the metaphor), you're going to create a very rough sketch of what goes on every page of your writing. Not the *detail* of those pages, but the *plan* for those pages.

I call this the Focus Plan.

And with it, you'll race through your writing.

So how does it work? It's pretty simple, really.

Start with the broad strokes. First, take your Preview, and determine roughly where each element will go in the final project. Then, zoom in on the detail, and elaborate each point, and sketch out your Plan. And then, finally, magnify it right down to the page level, and sprinkle your ideas onto each page.

Let's use this book as an example, since you've got it in your hands.

My Preview for this book was a one-page overview that basically outlined the FAST System. I wanted to show "how to write anything with lightning speed" by breaking down the FAST System into its component parts.

The first thing I did was decide on the end result. It would be a book, it would be 192 pages long, with 18 ten-page chapters.

Then I went to the micro level. I broke each chapter into ten segments. They're the little bold headings you see. And then (and this is the real power of this system), I listed two to five things I'd cover *in each section*.

I mapped out the broad strokes by putting the idea's major movements (in my case, the six sections) into their own defined space. And then I zoomed in to break it down even further.

The whole thing took about six hours, over two days. When it was done, I had a sharply focused Plan for writing this book.

Which enabled me to write it FAST.

Decide the End Result

The very first thing you'll need to do is decide on the end result. By that I mean, *what will it look like when it's done?*

Here's where your Preview comes in handy.

Visualize your Preview stretched out over the length of the Grid. You might have sections you can see clearly. But there's a lot of empty space, right? The idea doesn't cover it yet, does it?

That's what you do now — *before* you start writing!

Begin by deciding on your outcome. For *this* book, it was the FAST System, broken down into six sections (Setup, Focus, Apply, Strengthen, Tweak, Payoff). At this point, I didn't know much more than that.

If you were writing *Shawshank*, your "end result" might be a story with three major sections (1. Andy goes to prison, 2. Andy becomes a fixture of the system, and 3. life on the outside). That's the overall ride.

Then, as you start to see the picture more clearly in your mind, lay that out over the grid.

Use Setup and Payoff to help break down your idea. For *Shawshank*, we might give 25% to the beginning (he goes to prison), 50% to the middle (becomes a fixture), and 25% to the end (life outside). Now we have the broad strokes.

This book had six equal sections. Suddenly, the idea is clear.

And remember, *everything* you're doing right now can be changed later. If you're bouncing between two different ideas, just choose one.

Pick one, and keep moving forward. You're about to write this thing so fast, you could always chuck it out completely and do it all again, if you wanted to. And you'd *still* have it finished in less time than the old way of writing.

So once you've made your decision, it's time for some math.

Do a Little Math (Just a Little)

When I decided to publish this book, I had to learn all about ISBN numbers and cataloguing information with the National Library of Australia. On every form I had to file, I was asked for the page number of my book.

Well, I didn't know yet. It wasn't written yet.

So I did some math.

Six sections, three chapters each. If each chapter is ten pages, that makes 180 pages. Add the introduction and epilogue, and I've got 192 pages.

Sounds good to me! Thirty pages should be enough time to explain each section. And that's how I arrived at my page count.

It was entirely arbitrary. It was an accident.

But it turned out to be the best discovery I've made, and the secret to breaking down your writing! Because by assigning your work a page count, you can see the overview.

For example, let's say you wanted to write a thousand-page novel. You've got a story with five families and dozens of events that intertwine. You want each chapter to be short. Five pages or less. And you want each family to have equal time.

With this approach, you simply divide a thousand (pages) by five (families), which leaves 200 pages for each family. If you want five-page chapters, divide 200 (pages per family) by 5 (pages per chapter), and you've got 40 chapters for each family.

Now you can deliberately map each family's trajectory, by placing the chapters in an interesting order.

Suddenly you're in control.

And that's the beauty of this approach.

Some chapters might go longer or shorter. And maybe you'll adjust it as you write.

But by having that guide, suddenly your writing takes on a whole new energy. You're no longer writing a thousand-page novel. You're just knocking out a five-page chapter each day.

It makes the entire process of writing *doable*.

I call it "chunking."

Structure and Chunking

Chunking is the art of breaking down your idea into chunks.

Technically, you were "chunking" even back when you were stretching your idea across the grid, and deciding how many pages to devote to each major section.

But when you think of Chunking, I want you to focus on the *content* of your writing.

Specifically, ask yourself how each section will break down, and lay each chunk over its part of the grid.

Let me continue the example using this book.

We know I've got eighteen ten-page chapters for *Writing FAST*. That's the general plan. And chunking is the process of breaking it into chunks. Of deciding exactly what each of those chapters will be.

So I started with the four main sections — Focus, Apply, Strengthen, Tweak. I labeled each Chapter with a simple title. Something to tell me what's gonna go there. For the Focus section, it's "Capture Your Idea," "Make Your Idea Specific," and "Turn Your Idea into a Plan". (The "lightning rod" analogy came later, out of the book's subtitle, so I put this chapter's original title as the Focus section subtitle.)

Then I broke each chapter into chunks. For this chapter, it was "The Lightning Rod," "Create a Power Grid," "Broad strokes to Micro strokes," etc.

By doing this for the *whole book*, I made the writing process ten times easier. By giving each chunk one page, I immediately knew what would go on *every page* of my book. Not the details, yet, but the overview. The Plan.

How long does this take? It varies.

I'm not gonna lie to you, either. A longer, more complex project (like a thousand-page novel), might take several days or weeks. You could even take *months* if you wanted to. It depends on you, your style, your temperament.

But the more clearly you nail this step, the faster the rest of your writing will become. That thousand-page novel could take three *years* the old way. By chunking it properly, you could have your Plan in a few days or a couple weeks, and then blast through it in a few short months.

That's the power of the FAST System.

Fill in the Details

But if you really want to get into speed writing — if you really want to achieve lightning speed — the secret is to zoom in one more level.

Because even a single page can slow you down.

Now I'll admit something. Don't tell anyone I said this (people that don't read this book don't have to know), but I *frequently* skip this step. I'm so impatient, that by the time I get here, I just want to dive in. I can't wait anymore. I hate writing, and I'm dying to get it over with.

And *every* time I skip it, I regret it. *Every* time I skip it, my writing takes substantially longer than it needed to.

So here's what I recommend. I've found it works best to create two to five "points" for each chunk.

In other words, depending on what's going on the page, jot down two to five *different* ideas. Things to talk about *on* that page. For example, in *this* section ("Fill in the Details"), I've written "create detail for each page", "two to five points per chunk", and "kickstart the idea." That way, I have a plan.

All the other words you're reading in this section come *as I'm writing it* (during the Apply phase, or later). But by having those points listed for this section, I know exactly what I'm going to write here. Even if I can only devote ten or twenty minutes to my writing today, I can easily pick up where I left off tomorrow.

By taking your details to this level, you give your Left-brain (the logical side) a chance to *contribute* to the writing of this thing. And you won't ever go more than a paragraph or two without knowing what comes next.

Lightning Rod Boosters

The point here is *not* to make your writing rigid. It's to give you a roadmap. Writing is partly a process of discovery, and you need to have a way to re-incorporate what you discover.

So we'll also add what I call "booster areas" to the plan.

See, I realized that — just like in fiction writing — it's completely natural for your mind to invent fantastic ideas along the way. Things you can't plan for at the Focus stage of the process. Even if you nail exactly what's gonna go on every single page, I guarantee you this — it will change later.

It changes because your mind is active. And when you're writing, great ideas will pop into that head of yours. Most of the ideas will throw you off course. But some of the ideas will actually help you write *better*.

So plan for them.

At various points along the way, create space for yourself. Create areas of your Plan where you intentionally *don't* map it out. I didn't do it for this book (I didn't know to), but if I had it to do again, here's what I'd do.

For each chapter, I'd leave a section blank. And I'd label it "the discovery". And in each section, I'd write what I discovered at that point in the process.

That way, during the Apply phase — when all the lightning bolts are flying around and being channeled through the rod into the grid — I'd have an outlet for that random magic.

When you *give* yourself that opening, it has an amazing way of thrusting your work forward in a dramatic leap.

Remember, the magic of writing *does* appear when you're writing FAST.

Be sure to give yourself the opportunity to harness it.

Be sure to make it a part of your Plan.

Your Focus Plan in 5 Easy Steps

The Focus Plan is your lightning rod that harnesses your ideas. And you'll have it after applying these five easy steps.

1. <u>Decide on your end result</u>.
   If you start mapping before you know your idea, you'll end up creating a fragmented piece of writing. So decide on the outcome. Know your idea, and its shape. Then:

2. <u>Determine the page count</u>.
   It's completely arbitrary, and there's no right or wrong. It can change later. But for now, come up with a number. It'll get you going, and give you a target to work towards. Once you've got it, then:

3. <u>Divide it into chunks</u>.
   Broad strokes first. Use your Preview as your guide, and determine the major sections or movements of what you're writing. If your writing calls for a specific format, use it. Use Setup and Payoff. Then:

4. <u>Flesh out each level's details</u>.
   Break each major section down into smaller sections. Label those. Then break each of those into smaller sections, and label them. All the way down to individual pages. List 2 - 5 details for each page. You're "pre-writing." Take your time. It's worth it. Then:

5. <u>Add booster areas</u>.
   Give yourself areas within the writing to use the electricity you generate *during* the writing. Plant trigger words that are drawn from your story or your idea.

Don't be in a rush at this stage. It may seem like you're actually writing *slower* by taking all this extra time to map out your idea.

You're not. You're actually giving yourself a customized roadmap made especially for you. You can spot problems long before you start writing. And you can even test your ideas on readers to see if they work.

And so...

This chapter is about creating your Focus Plan.

If you follow these instructions, you'll have an incredibly detailed roadmap for your writing. And this is the cornerstone of the FAST System.

When you want to write FAST, you need to know where you're going. That way, you stay on track while you're writing.

As with everything else, don't get stuck on this. Yes, you'll absolutely need to devote _time_ to this step — the more, the better (to a point).

But if your end result is clear, it's also possible to chunk out each chapter, and write as you go.

For example, as I wrote this book, I realized I didn't put enough detail into my Focus Plan. So when I got to each chapter, I would take ten or fifteen minutes Focusing it. So I'd Focus, then Apply. Then get to the next chapter. Then Focus, then Apply. Then the next chapter... and so on.

Remember, these are not rules to slow you down and make your writing rigid. It's a system and methods to speed everything up, and free you.

By seeing your project laid out in front of you, with a Power Grid hovering over it... by imagining that brain storm over your work with lightning shooting out in all directions... by seeing that lightning rod attached to the Grid to harness your imagination...

By seeing, and grasping, and feeling the power of that, you can't help but unleash the power of your mind.

See?

I _knew_ you'd love it.

A [APPLY]

Turn Your Plan into Words

66 How do I know
what I think
until I see what I say? **99**

—E. M. Forster

7 Talktation: The New Art of Speed Writing

I love this part. Ready for some fireworks?

By now, you should have your Focus Plan laid out in front of you. What form it takes is up to you.

For this book, I created an outline on the computer. Each section was a heading, each chapter was a subheading (with page numbers listed next to them), and each segment *within* each chapter was a *sub*-subheading.

Then two to five details were listed under each of those.

But you could just as easily sketch it out on paper. Say, one sheet for each chapter. Or you could use a diagram on a whiteboard. Or, if you're good at drawing, maybe you could do an illustration of the grid?

For me, the outline worked. My Plan was pretty thorough. It changed along the way (they *always* do), but it also showed me exactly where I was going.

With it, I could stand at that observatory, and look out over the Power Grid. I could see the whole project in my mind, before I ever stepped foot on Page One.

If you haven't done that Focus Plan, *please* go back and do it. I want you to feel what I'm feeling.

Because I've got this excitement — this electricity — pumping through my veins right now. I'm so excited about writing this chapter, you probably wouldn't believe it. Really. I feel kinda stupid saying it, but I'm *alive* with anticipation.

And the reason is simple. I know exactly what I'm going to

write, I'm eager to get it on the page, and I know I'll *have* it on the page within a couple short hours!

It's an incredibly empowering feeling. And it's exactly the feeling I want *you* to experience. Because I know — I *know!* — that as soon as you experience it, you'll dive into everything you ever write.

What seemed like an impossible never-ending *chore*, has suddenly become *enjoyable*.

This first segment alone would've taken me about an hour to write, the old way. But I've just written it in six minutes (with an extra four minutes [make that nine] of tweaking in the Tweak phase). I'm trying to write the rest of the chapter in two hours. I'll let you know how I do.

And then maybe you'll feel it, too.

The Objective of this Phase

Put yourself in a different frame of mind.

Last section was all about creating the Focus Plan. That Plan is a combination Left-brain/Right-brain exercise. You used your Right-brain for some of it. It conjured up the details, and sparked ideas to put into the Power Grid.

But overall, that phase was predominantly Left-brain. You analyzed it. Thought it through. Planned the best way to present your idea. You would create a section heading, and give it a title. And then you'd step back, look at it, squint, and decide to rearrange the sections to make them flow better.

Well, this section is different. This section is as Right-brained as you can get. In fact, the more Right-brained you can make it, the better it will be.

See, you *know* where you're going now. The road is clear. Now we race down that road at lightning speed.

A is for Apply.

And the Apply phase is where you *apply* your plan. You turn that Focus Plan into words.

The objective of this phase is to get your words on the page *as fast as humanly possible*. In fact, I'm going to emphasize something you *think* you already understand. But I know for certain, you *don't* understand it yet. (I know because I didn't, either.)

It's this: The faster you get your words on the page, the better.

Yeah. I know you know that.

But stop nodding your head for a moment. I want you to really take a minute. Ponder that thought.

Truly grasp it.

The faster you get your words on the page, the better.

Don't skim over it. This idea has to burn inside you. Feel it like a fire in your belly. The faster you get your words on the page, the better. The faster the better. The *faster*, the *better!*

Why? Because your mind is a much better communicator than you give it credit for. You'll write with amazing clarity when you match the speed of your thoughts.

What is "speed writing"?

Speed writing is the act of writing quickly. There's no need to complicate it. It's just that simple.

When I decided to write this book, I searched the internet for information about speed writing. I didn't want to write a book that had already been written. But what I found was incredibly disappointing. It was all the same old stuff.

Traditionally, speed writing has centered around one exercise. Typically, you take three random words that have nothing to do with each other. You set the timer. And then you write as fast as you can for five minutes. You must include each of the three words within your work.

Pretty simple, right?

I've been doing a similar exercise in my screenwriting work-shops ever since I started. Instead of three random words, I'd ask you to pick an inanimate object somewhere in the room. (And you're not allowed to pick *me*, even if I *am* having a bad day.)

And then you write as fast as possible until I say stop.

It's great fun. Participants write furiously for about a minute or two. Then they start thinking. And then they slow down. And then they re-read what they've written.

Before you know it, they've stopped altogether.

Well, in a workshop, I can hover over you and *make* you continue. I even joke about it. I whisper (loudly) "No thinking" and "Keep going" and "No re-reading."

In a book, however, I can only *tell* you what to do and trust you to do it. Unfortunately, if you try doing this *without* someone hovering over you, it's so incredibly easy to let your brain get in the way. You'll stop for any old reason.

And that's why I've come up with a solution to try and chip away at your resistance.

But before we get to it, I need you to understand *why* this is so crucial.

Connect with Your Mind

All writing is communication.

And your brain is an Idea Factory whose job is to spit out ideas. You want to communicate those ideas to your reader, right?

Well, the faster you write, the more directly you tap into the *source* of your ideas. The faster you write, the more *natural* your communication.

By writing with lightning speed — writing at the speed of your thoughts — your ideas pour out onto the page almost as quickly as you *think* them. And when you're in tune with your idea, and you keep up with its flow, you don't give it a chance to get muddled.

By speed writing, you stay focused on the end result — on the *purpose* of the communication.

Think about what happens when you *talk*. In a normal conversation, you don't focus on the words. You only care about whether the other person *understands* or not. You don't stop and correct yourself. You don't ponder your words as you say them (and you *know* what we think of people who do!).

The *communication* is more important than the words. The *point* is always the top priority when you talk.

But when you slow down and *write*, you have too much time to think. You detach from the *point* you're communicating, and focus on *words*. And as you do, your mind gets flooded with extraneous ideas.

For example, take this section. My idea is "connect with your mind." I've got to get that idea across to you.

But if I don't stay focused, every little stray idea that pops into my head *as* I'm writing threatens to throw me off course.

Our Idea Factories bubble over with so many ideas, we'll get lost in a sea of "better ideas" if we're not careful!

Speed writing allows you to connect with your target, and drive in a straight line toward the end result.

You write so fast, you almost don't even have *time* to get lost. Your *objective* stays intact all the way through. By speed writing, you stay succinct. You plow forward, eyes locked on the goal.

You connect with your mind. You work *together*.

Keep Up with the Lightning

The whole struggle with writing is maintaining that focus.

When you *start* writing, you've got a clear idea of what you're trying to achieve. But you get halfway in, and you do what you always do (we're all guilty of it).

You slow down. You re-read your writing *as* you're writing it. And before you know it, your over-active Idea Factory starts pumping out *new* ideas, throwing you in whole new directions!

For example, let's say I'm writing these words right now (which, funnily enough, I am!). But I throw in that little humorous quip, and then I'm not sure if it's the right choice.

So I stop writing, and go back to re-read this section. I'm trying to get a sense of the flow, or to "get back into the rhythm."

Well, if my idea isn't clear, I'm gonna lose focus immediately. Some stray lightning bolt will shoot out in a different direction every time. Maybe it's because I judged my work. Maybe I had a better idea. Or maybe just a *different* idea. The fact is, it's almost impossible to *avoid* these distractions if you re-read it!

I get to the third paragraph up there, and the idea of "slowing down" sparks another idea — about, say, what happened last chapter when I slowed down, and how I spent six solid hours pulling my hair out because of it.

Well, that might be a valuable tidbit, but it doesn't maintain the focus. It doesn't help me get to my point. It muddles me up. Because now I've got a section with *two* valuable tidbits. Suddenly, I have to decide which one's better. Which one's right? Which one's more effective?

But I'm not in the Tweak phase yet! I'm not even in the Strengthen phase! My brain is a perfectionist, and if I give it that inch, it'll take a mile — and it'll stop me dead in my tracks until I fix that paragraph.

And I'll spend the rest of the afternoon re-reading my material to *decide* which one's better!

All because I didn't write fast enough.

All because my brain fires off those lightning bolts a little bit too quickly for my fingers to handle.

All because I couldn't keep up with the lightning.

You can go ahead and nod again. Because I know it happens to you, too.

Introducing Talktation

So how do we get past this problem?

Simple. Talktation.

Now I need to make one thing perfectly clear. Talktation is partly conceptual, and partly practical.

What the heck does *that* mean?

It means that in order to *do* it, you've got to get your mind around it first.

Here's the idea:

No matter how fast you type (or hand-write), you'll never be as fast as your mind. It's just not possible. Your mind goes at lightning speed. But *literally* at lightning speed. And human fingers simply can't move that fast. They never will. It defies the laws of physics.

Your mind will *always* outrun your fingers. Always.

But with Talktation, we're going to train your mind and your fingers to work in sync with each other.

At first, it will mean *slowing down your thought* to match your typing speed. But once they're in sync, you can increase the speed of your thought, and your fingers will follow. It's very cool.

Here's one way to get your mind around the concept.

Have you ever seen a small child reading a book? Heck, even adults do it, too. As they read the book, they mouth the words. It's as if they're speaking each word to themselves in order to understand it.

It's an incredibly *sloooooow* way to read. In fact, the whole technique of speed *reading* starts by forcing yourself to *stop* that. If you focus on each individual word as you read it, you're reading a lot slower than you could be.

But to apply Talktation, that's exactly what we *want* to do.

The process is simple.

Focus on each word *as you type it*. Then focus on the next word *as you type it*. And then the next. And the next...

So let's take *this* sentence as an example. To use Talktation, I would focus on the word "So" as I type it. Then I'd focus on "let's" as I type it. Then "take" as I type it... and so on.

It goes quickly, but you type each word *as* you think it. In fact, you don't even *think* the next word in the sentence until you've typed the last one.

Another way to understand it is to understand what it's *not*. You *don't* think "So, let's take this sentence as an example" and then type it. You don't let the *whole* sentence form before you type. And you don't let yourself even *think* of what the next paragraph will be while you're writing *this* one.

Instead, you focus only on the word... you're... writing... right... now. Keep... your... attention... on... each... word... as... you're... writing... it. And *type* it (or hand-write it) as the thought moves through your mind.

In other words, *synchronize* your *thoughts* with your *fingers*.

Talk it Onto the Page

When you're first using the Talktation technique, it helps to say each word out loud. Think of writing as *talking* onto the page.

They're really no different, y'know. One form of communication (writing) is written; the other (talking) is verbal. They're two sides to the same coin.

The only difference is *time*.

When we listen to someone talk, we excuse a lot of sloppy communication. Notice how often people say "um" and "uhh." Or how they go through stray ideas on their way to the point.

But we forgive that when we talk. Why? Because when we talk, we're closer to the speed of thought. And thoughts don't come out perfectly formed. And we *know* that. So it's okay. And you give the speaker some leeway.

But we wouldn't forgive it in writing! Written communication took *time* to get to you. Think of the *time* between my *writing* this book, and you *reading* it. Time has passed! And since time has passed, the reader assumes there's been enough time to weed out all those mistakes. (And you will — later!)

But that *time* is the only difference between writing and talking. You *have* time to fix it later. For now, *talk* your words onto the page. Get them there as quickly as possible!

When you get your head around Talktation — talking your words onto the page, your fingers in sync with your thoughts — it will literally revolutionize your writing.

The Speed of Your Keys

And no doubt about it, Talktation improves with your typing speed, and with practice.

So I want to make a little case for learning how to type. If you don't know how to type, trust me, it's the best thing a writer can learn how to do.

Dictation just isn't the same. With dictation, you're detached from your writing. Someone else is transcribing your words (even if that someone is you). But writing *is* different to speaking. Your words *do* need to be presented differently. By learning to type (and type *fast*), you actually plug into your writing in a much more direct way.

My own typing speed is upwards of eighty words a minute. I don't say that to impress you (some readers will undoubtedly be *un*impressed), but to point something out to you.

The faster you can type, the closer you get to your thoughts. The faster you can type, the easier you make it on yourself.

In fact, I've noticed that when I really whip myself up into a writing frenzy — when I start a chapter the way I started this one, all pumped up and ready to power through it — my typing speed increases.

I've been able to hit up to a hundred words a minute when I write in that "zone." And you can do it, too. All it takes is practice. And you can practice *while* you write!

The point of Talktation is to get your fingers and your brain in sync, so you can keep your mind focused on your goal — and avoid shooting out in a million different directions.

The point is to speed write. *Effectively*.

Start slow. Practice. And then increase the speed.

When you're excited about your topic, you'll be amazed at how quickly your fingers fly alongside your thoughts.

Talktation in 5 Easy Steps

Talktation isn't *just* a concept — it's a physical technique that improves with practice. When you apply this technique to your Focus Plan, your writing will literally take off. It's an incredible rush. Try it. Here's how, in five easy steps.

1. <u>Plant the idea in your head</u>.
   Start with a clear thought of what you're trying to write. Focus on a specific *outcome* you want to reach. This will help you stay focused as you get your fingers and brain to sync up. Then:

2. <u>Match your *thought* to your typing</u>.
   Not the other way around! This is the biggest mistake writers make. You can't just speed up your typing because you want to. Instead, as you begin typing, *slow down your thoughts*, so you can synchronize the two, and then:

3. <u>Talk your words onto the page</u>.
   Think slowly and deliberately, and type each word *as* you think or speak it. Don't let your typing get ahead of your thoughts, or vice versa. Think a word, type it. Think a word, type it. Word. Type it. Then, gradually:

4. <u>Increase your thought speed</u>.
   Word. Type it. Word, type it. Word type it. Word-type-it. WordTypeIt. Wortypit. Get the idea? As you increase thought speed, don't go faster than you can type. Let your typing speed gradually increase. Keep them in sync. Then:

5. <u>Practice, and practice some more</u>.
   The more you do this, the faster you'll get. Don't practice on disconnected writing exercises. Practice on the project you're writing! Why not kill two birds with one stone?

Talktation is the technique that will turn you into a blazing fast writer. Practice on the short-form writing (like your emails, your letters, your notes), and perfect it on the long-form writing. Take every opportunity you can to practice it, and watch your speed skyrocket.

And so...

I absolutely love this technique. And remember how I told you I wanted to write this chapter in two hours?

Well, it's taken me two hours and six minutes. And that included a seven minute telephone interruption. And a ten minute break, thanks to that little flashing icon on my email inbox. (I gotta learn to shut that thing off while I'm writing.)

And this from the World's Pickiest Perfectionist!

Not bad, huh?

(Just to follow up, I've also spent an additional three hours on this chapter during the Strengthen and Tweak phases. And I'll also readily admit that this was the most quickly-written chapter in the whole book. Just goes to show ya. Excitement has a way of energizing your work.)

Talktation is the key to taking your Focus Plan, and getting it on the page as quickly as possible. It's a simple conceptual technique you can start mastering with the very next words you write.

In the next chapter, we'll look at what to do with that overflowing brain of yours, and how to keep yourself focused. Because even Talktation can't keep that Factory from pumping out ideas.

And then in the following chapter, I'll show you how to apply Talktation to your Focus Plan and "ride the wave" to the finish line.

Writing has never been this fun. Wouldn't you agree?

8 Harness Your Idea Overflow

The beauty of writing FAST is that the faster you write, the faster you'll write. That's not a riddle. It's a fact.

Your writing feeds on itself. Speed fuels more speed.

The problem is that you've got too many ideas, and each one sparks another, which throws you off on stray tangents.

It's always the same. Even with the Talkation technique.

You sit down to begin "blasting through" your work, but you end up in the middle of nowhere, lost and confused, and convinced that writing is better left to foolhardy authors who can just *keep* their stupid mysterious aristocracy.

No!

In this chapter, we'll harness that overflow, and keep you on track. I'll show you a simple technique to make sure you never get lost again.

A way to stay focused on your target, while your mind is swirling.

And I know what I'm talking about here. I've got a very long history of coming up with one "brilliant" idea after another. And the techniques in this chapter have saved my sanity.

It's not just talk.

See, you might know this stuff already. You might think, *Yeah yeah, I've gotta stay focused*. We've heard it all before.

But until you *can* stay focused and make it all the way through your writing, you don't really *know* it. Not in your gut. And *that's* where you need to understand it.

Staying focused is the key to writing fast. Keeping your mind clear of distractions (both outside — like my blinking email icon [hang on while I check that] — and *inside*, like your thoughts themselves) is absolutely essential.

And that's what this chapter is all about.

Keeping you on track, when your mind is working overtime.

Non-linear Overflow

Last chapter, we talked about how the speed of your fingers will never match the speed of your mind.

With Talkation, you'll write fast. But your Idea Factory will always be faster.

Remember, this thing is cranking out idea after idea after idea. Each one sparks the next, in an endless chain of thought.

But here's the problem.

Your mind is *not* organized like a book. A book is linear. You start on Page One, and read each subsequent page to the end. The ideas build on top of each other. And as they do, a picture — the idea of the book — forms in your mind.

But your mind doesn't work like that. Nope.

Your mind is *non-linear*. It's a mesh of neural pathways. There's no "Point A to Point B." If I throw out the word *yellow*, and give you a moment to free associate it, your mind will go in about sixteen different directions *at the same time*. A lemon. A car. A flower. Teeth. A friend named Yolanda.

But those ideas aren't *building*. They're *linked* by association. By the common thread. In this case, "yellow."

Your mind forms pictures by grabbing those links and locking them together. But *how* the ideas are linked depends on the thought, and what it means *to you*. In *your* mind.

Well that's great for *us*. It allows us to think laterally. It fuels imagination. It helps us draw meaning out of our ideas and our memories.

But we certainly can't *write* that way!

The reader can't follow our non-linear train of thought. (What does Yolanda have to do with *yellow*?!). Because the reader's mind is moving in a *different* non-linear direction!

Those stray thoughts are for you. To make the idea clear to *your* mind. But to transfer that idea into your *reader's* mind, you've got to keep it linear. You've got to build that idea. You've got to stay focused.

And when you can't stay focused, it's the stray idea that throws you off course. I call it "Overflow."

It might not be a *bad* idea — heck, it might be exactly what you need! — but you'd better not let it get in the way, or your writing will get very very stuck.

Too Many Ideas

Your brain's just trying to help.

It doesn't know any better. It sees you writing about that topic, and it wants to contribute. It wants to be useful! It's like a little kid that desperately wants to help Dad in the garage. He keeps handing him the wrong tools. He keeps getting in the way. But you know he means well.

If you don't blast straight through your writing, from the very first page to the very last, your Idea Factory is going to interrupt.

A lot.

With more ideas than you can shake a stick at.

And the only way you're going to get through it is to gently tell your brain you *appreciate* it. "Thank you for that wonderful idea, Brain."

And then promptly ignore it. And get back to the work at hand. (If you don't say Thank-you, your brain will gradually stop giving you ideas. And that can't be a good thing. Be polite and keep the relationship friendly as long as possible.)

Keep your eyes focused on the road ahead.

I know it sounds a little counter-intuitive. You've got all these great ideas popping into your mind, and here I am suggesting you ignore them. What if they're great ideas? What if they're the missing link between that Focus Plan and whatever it is that will really make this thing rock?

We'll get to that in a minute.

For now, just don't buy into the sales pitch.

Not every one of those ideas will be as valuable as the Oscar-winner claims they'll be. Not every idea is worth the time it takes to ponder it.

But *every* single one of those ideas will push you off the rails. And cause a major wreck. Even the good ones.

Personal Interference

Take this scenario. It used to happen to me all the time.

You sit down to start writing. You have an idea of where you're going. Maybe you have a detailed Focus Plan, or maybe just a sketch and a hunch.

And you start typing.

You write a paragraph. And just to be sure your paragraph doesn't completely suck, you re-read it.

But when you re-read it, you notice you misspelled a word. No biggie. You fix it, and then re-read it again.

Only... you notice that your word choice makes the first half of that sentence kinda clunky. If you just remove this word, and slide that phrase over there, that oughtta do it. Yeah, that's better. You re-read it again.

Okay, yeah, I think that's pretty good. But — hey — that gives me an idea!

And you run with the idea. You get another two paragraphs written before you stop. But you're not sure what you've got. So you do the same thing again.

These new paragraphs require a couple little modifications, too. But it's no problemo. Change this, tuck that, nip that over there, and presto! It's all looking pretty good.

You re-read the three paragraphs.

Only — hang on — you had an idea, didn't you? It was the reason you wrote those second two paragraphs. Wait a minute. Hang on. You *did* have an idea. You're sure of it.

What the heck *was* it again? Something about... no, umm... gawd, I'm really not sure anymore.

You re-read it again. And again. And again. You can't remember the original idea, but a *new* idea pops into your head.

That one should tie it back together! So you run with it for a couple paragraphs, when you do the same little fix-it routine.

But now when you re-read your page, you've forgotten what you even *started out* trying to say! You've got six little tangents reaching out like a crooked branch on a dead tree. The original direction is lost, but so are each of the *new* ideas!

It's Personal Interference. It's *you* getting in your *own* way! Stop that!

Focus on the Road Ahead

I'm going to repeat something. You've heard it before, but we all keep forgetting it (me, too!), so I'll repeat it again.

Focus on the target. And under *no* circumstances should you even *think* about re-reading your work until you've got *everything* on the page. Seriously! Don't look back!!

Listen. Writing is a process. Writing is a *process*. Writing. What is it? That's right. It's a *process!* It's not an activity. Typing is not writing. Writing is the *process!*

What does this mean?

It means that when you stop and re-read your work, you will always — *always* — slow yourself down. For absolutely no good reason whatsoever.

You can fix it later.

Writers get stuck when they forget that. And, let's face it, it's the best thing *about* writing — the fact that you can fix it later!

When you say something in person, you don't have that luxury. There's no time. Unless you're quick on your feet and have sharp verbal communication skills, talking is *always* more hazardous than writing.

When you write something that reads poorly, you can fix it. Correct it. Change it. Modify it. Perfect it. Hone it. Sharpen it. Adjust it. Tweak it...

So for crying out loud, let yourself go! Do that stuff *later* in the process. Do that stuff when we get to the Tweak section.

Don't do it now!

Keep your eyes on the target. Write as fast as you can. Get the words on the page. That's *this* part of the process.

And when ideas pop into your mind, chuck them in the BIN!

Throw Your Ideas in the BIN

When I was a kid, I had a wonderfully active imagination. I always dreamed I would grow up to be a huge movie star. Whatever shows I was watching on television, I had invented characters for myself.

I was Sam's long-lost son on *Cheers*. I was Alice's *other* son on *Alice*. I was Nancy McKeon's boyfriend on *The Facts of Life*.

I was Dr Caldwell's nephew on *St Elsewhere*. (As you can see, I would always be related to the central characters, so I'd have a regular part instead of some guest appearance. Even as a kid, I knew the value of a steady gig.)

My little imagination ran rampant. I used to carry around a notebook to put all my ideas in. I called it my "Big Idea" notebook.

I would jot down storylines, and crazy ideas. I would put doodles in there, and poems (oh, I was quite the poet), and whatever short stories came to mind.

I stopped carrying around that notebook when I became a teenager. After all, it wasn't very cool. And I couldn't be a dork, could I? (I turned out to be a dork after all, but at least I wasn't carrying a notebook.)

It's a shame I didn't hold onto that old thing.

Because it's absolutely the *best* way to capture your ideas.

Remember, ideas are slippery. If you don't capture them while they're in your face, they'll be gone a few minutes later.

Well, I've returned to that tool.

And I call it the BIN. Your own "Big Idea Notebook."

Think of it as a recycling bin. It's a place to chuck something that might get used later.

Here's how to use it.

When you're writing, keep two files open on the computer. One is the file you're working on. Right now, mine is the page I'm typing these words into. But in the background is an open, empty file. It's my BIN.

(You could also keep a blank sheet of paper by your side.)

If a stray idea pops into your head, quickly switch over to that page, jot the idea down, and come back here and continue writing. That way, you won't lose those few "big ideas" that *are* valuable. But you won't get sidetracked by the ones that *aren't* either!

Remember, you'll only get through your writing *fast* if you focus on the target and write as fast as you can. Slowing down for even a moment will let the Overflow rush in.

Don't let it happen!

Throw those ideas into the BIN, and get back to your writing. You can decide later what to do with them.

Maybe you'll empty the BIN. Maybe you'll recycle. For now, just chuck stray ideas in there, and get back to your writing.

The BIN is deceptively simple. It really doesn't seem like a breakthrough technique. But the faster you write (especially when you start applying Talktation), the more powerful it becomes. You've given yourself a way to stay focused.

Grow the Idea Tree

Now, depending on how well you stay on target, you might end up with a lot of ideas in your BIN.

The first thing you'll notice is that many of these stray ideas are similar or related. Some have a natural progression, and some grow out of what you've already got on the page.

Think of them as being part of a tree. Connect the dots. Create branches for each of them, and *link* the ideas that are somehow connected.

In order to use them, you need to see *how* they connect.

If the connection is *obvious*, grow this Idea Tree *as* you drop ideas into the BIN. But if it's not, come back and grow the tree later. Remember, you're doing this *as* you're blasting words onto the page. Don't dwell on it. Stay focused on your original target.

My Idea Tree usually ends up as an outline, because for *my* brain, that seems to be the easiest way to organize these stray thoughts.

But maybe you'd rather draw a sketch on a piece of paper. (That's how I discovered the Idea Tree in the first place.) You take the idea, and put it in the middle of the page. And then you branch connecting ideas off the main one. And smaller ideas off those. And so on. Until you have what looks exactly like a tree.

Gradually, you'll train your mind to organize your stray ideas the instant they pop up. But always start slow. Take it nice and easy, and get comfortable with it.

The best way grow the Idea Tree is when you take breaks from your writing. You won't distract yourself from your target. You can approach it with a clear head.

And you break the *process* of writing into manageable chunks (which is the whole point of the FAST System!).

When you take the extra time, you might find a *theme* growing out of this Idea Tree. Something you *need* in your writing. Maybe something you forgot to include in your Focus Plan.

It happens to me all the time. By harnessing it, you won't forget to include it. And you help yourself strengthen your writing.

Your brain talks to you. It has all the answers you need.

It's up to you to listen.

Recycle for a Boost

And then, finally, you recycle it.

When you fleshed out your Focus Plan in Chapter 6, you left booster areas. You gave yourself a way to include what you discovered along the way.

This is what goes in those booster areas. Your Overflow.

For most of the time I've been writing — and *all* of the time I've been teaching — I've always believed that part of the magic of writing was in the discovery.

I hated the idea of planning everything out.

I thought if you *did*, you'd never allow yourself the magic of that discovery. You'd miss those moments that bring writing to life. Those awesome moments where you're right in the middle of a sentence and — aha! — something fires off in your brain and *charges* your writing.

It invigorates you, and excites you! You feel it in your bones. And all because you made that discovery in that very moment.

That's the magic of writing.

And I believe in it now more than ever. Because now I can explain it.

When you let go, your Idea Factory connects with the page *directly*. You're not letting your conscious Left-brain Movie Critic get in the way of that flow. The *magic* comes from harnessing those lightning bolts, and putting them back in your work.

And guess what. Your writing *must* include those spontaneous discoveries — those ideas you harness *as* you write. If it doesn't, the reader will know it. There won't be any life to it.

By creating a Focus Plan, nailing down your idea, keeping a BIN by your side to harness the overflow, and blasting through your writing as fast as you can, you let magic happen.

And what isn't *on* the page, will be waiting in the BIN. If you review it, and infuse it, you launch to the next level.

And that's magic.

And it happens by design.

5 Easy Steps to Harness the Overflow

Distractions sideline you, even if the distraction comes from your *own* great ideas. Here, then, are the five easy steps to harness the idea overflow.

1. Fix on the goal.
   Know your outcome before you start. If you don't, you'll have trouble knowing which ideas are part of the chunk you're working on, and which are distractions. If you're clear, then when the overflow happens, you'll:

2. Notice the stray idea.
   It's a stray idea if it doesn't directly push you towards the *immediate* goal. It might only be a slight diversion. But if you want to write FAST, you'll need to keep every distraction in check. Once you spot it, then:

3. Drop it in the BIN.
   Always, always, *always* write with a BIN by your side. It could be a sheet of paper or another file. You don't want to scramble to find one when an idea hits. Be prepared. Pop the stray idea into the BIN immediately, and then:

4. Shut it out and keep going.
   Hold onto your original train of thought. Once your idea is in the BIN, it's safe. You don't have to think about it anymore. So don't! Get right back into pushing towards your goal. Then:

5. Review your ideas later. When you're finished blasting through your pages, look for common themes in the ideas in your BIN. Grow your Idea Tree when you're on a break, and plug those stray ideas into your Booster areas.

By planning for and harnessing your idea Overflow, you'll quickly train your mind. You'll send a clear message to your Idea Factory — that when you sit down to write, you mean business.

Stray ideas can be incredibly valuable. This technique will help you grab them, while you power through your pages.

And so...

You've now got two great techniques for speed writing.

First was Talktation, and now is the BIN. Used together, and combined with your Focus Plan, it becomes surprisingly easy to get a chapter onto the page quickly and efficiently.

In the next chapter, we're going to tie these techniques together for the speed writing payoff.

But before we move on, I want to stress something.

These aren't just "things you can do." If you're still only *reading* this book (and not yet *applying* it), it's easy to dismiss these techniques as "good ideas."

They're more than "good ideas." They will help you write ten times faster than you've ever written before.

Earlier, we said that in order to really *feel* these ideas, you need to *experience* them.

Well, when you *read* this, you might think, *Yeah, that's cool — I can see how that could work.*

But that's not enough.

I'm flying through these chapters like never before. I'm actually excited about writing again. (And, honestly, for me, that is very bizarre.) I'm actually thinking I might write another book when I'm done!

And I'm the guy who always thought writing was *torturous*.

When you feel these things in your gut — when you really apply them and use them and *see* how they work — it will lift you to a whole new place.

So if you're just passively reading along, c'mon! Get started. Can't you see by now that the FAST System really works?

9 Ride Your Wave to the End

Imagine in your mind the rolling sound of thunder, somewhere off in the distance.

Hear the slow, steady hum. That dark and ominous sound, lifting off the horizon. Listen carefully, as it draws closer. The sound of the wind. The rumbling. The crackling.

In the distance, faint claps of thunder. Slowly approaching. Creeping towards us. Drawing up its energy.

And you can tell. It's getting close. Real close.

And then suddenly, unexpectedly, it strikes.

Like the fierce crack of a whip and the buzz of electricity flicking through a static coil. And *bang!* The bolt of lightning sends a bone-rattling crash reverberating outward in every direction, echoing across the quiet landscape.

And the landscape feels it. Absorbs it. Feeds off it.

That landscape is your Power Grid. And underneath it are your pages, strewn out end-to-end.

The bolt of lightning is your idea. Charged up. Energized. Ready to be grabbed and harnessed. Ready to electrify each page of your work.

It's not enough to see it. You've gotta *feel* it in your bones.

The last two chapters gave you techniques to write your pages as fast as you can. In this chapter, we're gonna grab hold of that lightning bolt, and use it to power through your work.

You've seen that power at your fingertips. Now it's time to *use* it. To pour your energy onto the page.

A Different Kind of Wave

You're about to begin Applying your Focus Plan.

And that means filling pages as quickly as possible. It means turning *blank* pages into pages with words on them.

It doesn't mean creating a masterpiece. It doesn't mean creating something that will move and entertain and hold your reader's attention.

No. That's too much pressure. Keep it simple, instead.

All you're doing is *filling blank pages with words*.

And I really want you to grasp this point. Because if you don't, you'll never get through it.

The Apply phase is *not* about writing "well." It's not about crafting a beautiful manuscript. It's about one thing, and one thing only. What is it? *Filling blank pages with words*.

Every single word could suck. Every single one! But when you're holding a stack of your own pages, you've done it right.

And the easiest way to do it, is to ride the wave.

The "riding the wave" metaphor comes from surfing. But when you think of *this* "riding the wave," picture a different kind of wave, instead. Picture of a wave of *energy*.

Writing is communication. And you're trying to get the idea from *your* head, into the *reader's* head.

Instinctively, you want to control it. Steer it. Guide it.

But when you *try*, you get in your own way.

No. Forget that. You've got three things to help you let go. You've got your Focus Plan. You've got Talktation. And you've got the BIN. You're ready. You're all set up to harness the lightning bolts. Now all you have to do is *let go and ride the wave*.

Understand this. Let this wave of energy just pour out of you and push you across the pages.

When you do, the whole process becomes almost effortless.

Chunking Pays Off

During the Focus phase of the FAST System, you applied the technique of "chunking." You took the idea in your mind, and you broke it down into little manageable chunks.

And you stretched those chunks over a number of pages.

Maybe each chunk is five pages. Or maybe ten. Or whatever you can blast through in one sitting.

Chunking is for *you*, not your reader. Chunking exists for one reason only — *to help you ride the wave.*

By breaking your writing into chunks, you've got a simple way of getting from Point A to Point B.

The first chunk might go from page 1 to page 5. Now that you've got Talktation and the BIN, you can leap right in! Write as fast as you can to page 5, and you're done.

Then jump into the next chunk. Page 5 to page 10. Write as fast as possible — dropping any stray ideas into the BIN. And then the next chunk.

And again with the next. And the next. And the next.

As you get better at Talktation, the wave gets easier to ride. The BIN keeps you from falling off. And the chunks keep you from getting tumbled.

Because the chunks are small and manageable, you stay focused on the target.

And you don't have to think about anything except filling the pages with words.

Write to Your Checkpoints

Each chunk in your plan is separated by two checkpoints.

These checkpoints allow you to seize an idea, get excited by it, and focus on a goal that's close enough to *reach*.

Here's how it works.

When you look at your Focus Plan, see the next checkpoint. Lock the *idea* in your mind. See the target. And then use Talktation to get there as fast as you can.

For example, in this chapter, each segment subheading is a checkpoint for me. When I look at my Focus Plan, *this* chunk is "write to your checkpoints." The next chunk is "find the optimal flow."

The end of this chunk is my checkpoint. When I've made the point — when I think I've been clear enough that *you* understand what I mean by "write to your checkpoints" — I've reached my checkpoint for this section.

It might not be graceful. It might not even be terribly effective. But I'm not worried about that right now.

All I care about is filling up this segment. I'll come back and fix it later. But by filling the pages as quickly as possible, I do the hardest thing a writer has to do: I put words on the page.

And that's *all* the Apply phase is about.

This chunk might take a page, or it might take two. I keep writing until I think I've made the point as best I can. And when I have, I've reached the checkpoint.

And I can move on.

Which would you rather write? A 192-page book, or a one-page chunk?

If you ride the *little* waves, you'll be floating along the *big* wave without even noticing it.

Find the Optimal Flow

Now, I've got to warn you of a potential hazard: Comparing speeds. Don't do it. Ever.

I've given you examples of how long it took me to write segments or chapters from this book. I've done it to *motivate* you. To *inspire* you. To show you it can be done!

But *your own speed will vary*.

In fact, you might write a hell of a lot faster than I do. Or you might also write considerably *slower*. That's okay!

Each of us is unique. We have something unique to say, and a unique journey we've taken through life.

Well, guess what? We also have a unique "optimal flow" — a writing speed that seems to suit us best.

Just because I wrote a chapter in two hours doesn't mean you can. Or even that you *should!* Trying for that speed is ridiculous. Don't even bother. That's *my* speed (and I've discovered it's not even my *optimal* speed!).

I bring this up because I don't want you to get discouraged.

I got *very* disappointed when I started on this book. I thought I'd be powering through ten pages every two hours. But when I kept falling behind, I'd sink into frustration.

I felt like a failure.

And the weight of the world on my shoulders began to crush me again. I wasn't writing "fast enough." And it made me judge my writing even more. And it slowed me down even further.

It's a never-ending downward spiral.

It's counter-productive. And such a waste of time!

Push yourself. Move as fast as you can. But if that's only a half-page a day, so be it! You'll write *faster* by consistently writing a half-page a day, than *unnaturally* trying to do ten pages a day, and getting stuck because you're beating yourself up.

When you tap into your optimal flow, you'll *ride* the wave. If you try for a speed that doesn't fit, you'll miss it every time.

Take the pressure off yourself. When you *do* find your optimal speed and plug into it, it just fits.

And you'll notice your speed gradually increase over time.

Take Breathers

As you apply your Focus Plan, even at the optimal speed, you need to take a breather from time to time. You're focused on an idea very intensely. Give your mind a break.

Remember Chapter 4? Well, there's something you should know about it.

I wrote it twice.

That's right. On my computer, I've got two separate versions of the same chapter.

Here's what happened.

I had been writing all day, and I hadn't stepped away from my computer in about twelve hours (!). It was before I wrote *this* section of the book, so while I "knew" all about how to turn my plan into words, I didn't really *know* it in my gut.

In the early evening, I'd nearly finished the first Chapter 4.

But when I read it back, my mind started playing tricks on me. I began over-thinking it. No, no, no. This line isn't right. Aw, that's so confusing. Jeez, this part over here is terrible.

I couldn't focus. I couldn't concentrate. I'd been staring at the screen for so long, I despised every word I had written.

My eyes were bleary. I was just tired of hearing myself talk.

At about nine o'clock at night, I freaked out. My writing was going nowhere, and I felt the weight of my deadline thundering down on me.

So I chucked the whole chapter out the window, and started again. I wrote quickly and furiously. And the words poured out of me. I made a huge revelation, and I was riding the wave. And it was awesome. I loved it. I felt like I had finally hit my stride.

I might even finish the book on time after all.

Well two days later, I re-read both versions of Chapter 4. And guess what I discovered.

They were *both* fine. Can you believe that? Both of them!

Now I had the added problem of having to *blend* two completely different chapters into one effective one! Arrrrrrgh.

If only I'd taken a break. I would've seen it all more clearly.

Writing at the speed we're writing, you're incredibly focused. You need to shake that off when you're done.

Or you won't see the forest for the trees.

Perfection is a Headspace

Please don't Tweak during the Apply phase. Please don't go for perfection.

The problem with perfection is that it's a figment of your imagination. There's no such thing.

What *you* consider perfection and what *I* consider perfection are two different things. But I'll go a step further. What you consider perfection *today* and what you *will* consider perfection at this time next *year* are *also* two different things!

Now, this is not permission to be sloppy. Your job is to communicate your idea as efficiently and effectively as possible.

But to strive for perfection — especially during the Apply phase — is an exercise in futility. Absolutely pointless.

Give yourself a strong, solid direction, and let yourself go.

That's all you need during this phase.

Get your words on the page. Tap into the flow. Harness the lightning bolt. Forget quality — go for *quantity*.

And smile as you write.

When I was doing radio and voice-over work as a teenager, I got some advice from the station manager at the radio station I worked for. It's advice I've never forgotten, and I believe it applies across the board to life itself.

She said, "When you speak into the microphone, always smile. It brings a smile to your words that listeners can physically *hear*." And it's true! It brightens the sound of your voice.

It brightens your writing, too.

Enjoy writing crap. And write it *fast*.

Riding the Wave in 5 Easy Steps

You've got the tools, and you're in the right frame of mind. It's time to turn your plan into words. Here are the five easy steps to get your words on the page with lightning speed.

1. <u>Determine your checkpoint</u>.
   Be clear on where you're going, or you'll slip off the rails mid-stream. Your Focus Plan has small, bite-sized chunks for you. Don't worry about anything but *this* chunk. Fix the checkpoint — the goal — in your mind, and then:

2. <u>Jump on the wave</u>.
   Use Talktation and keep your BIN handy, and blast as fast as you can towards that checkpoint. Remember: Don't steer it. Let it pour out of you. Make sure you:

3. <u>Don't think</u>.
   When you think, you judge. When you judge, you criticize. And when all you're trying to do is get words on the page, criticism is a complete waste of time. We'll do that later. For now, let go and *leap in!* Then:

4. <u>Find your speed zone</u>.
   Remember, it's not a race with anyone. There's only you. You have an optimal speed (which will change over time). Find it, plug into it, and ride it. And, then:

5. <u>Enjoy</u>.
   There's nothing better than tapping into your own creative energy and letting it carry you through your work. If you don't enjoy writing, you won't *do* it. When you enjoy it, you'll stop controlling it, and let it pour out of you.

Use these simple steps to apply your Focus Plan. Take your writing all the way through each of the chunks to the finish line. It's not difficult. But you must "let go."

You'll resist at first. Especially as you struggle to kill the Critic. He's a particularly ornery bugger. But he'll fade away when you put all your attention on making your idea clear.

Oh. And don't forget to smile. We can hear it.

And so...

We're just about to hit the halfway mark of this book.

For me as the writer, I'm over the moon. There's something incredibly satisfying about reaching this point. And you'll know exactly what I'm talking about when you reach this point on your own project.

If you've taken the time to create a solid Focus Plan, once you get to halfway, everything's about to get a whole lot easier.

But for now, I want to stress that we're only halfway there.

Don't worry what your words look like at this stage. Just get them onto the page. That's all the Apply section is about. It's not about making your work flawless. You can't do that right now. We *must* wait until later for that.

For now, we just ride the wave.

I hope you're enjoying the FAST System so far. I hope you can see how this will revolutionize your writing. (And if you can't see that yet, it only tells me you're not *experiencing* it!)

Listen carefully.

Can you hear the sound of the thunder?

It's churning in the sky. Ready. Willing. Waiting.

Finally. It's at your command.

[STRENGTHEN]

Turn Your Words into Gold

66 Books aren't written —
they're rewritten. **99**

—Michael Crichton

10 Inspect What You Have

Wow! You made it through! You didn't think you could, but you did. Towards the middle, you thought you were a goner. You almost gave up, even! But no. You persevered.

And you filled up all those blank pages!

Incredible.

Tell me this isn't the greatest feeling in the world!

Listen. Now that you're here, you've gotta do something. And it's absolutely *essential* if you're working on a long-form project.

You've got to *reward yourself.* Take yourself out to dinner. Go on a vacation somewhere. Buy a trinket. *Something.*

Because what you've done is really quite amazing. You have conquered what most writers agree is the hardest part of writing: Getting words on the page.

(Nobody needs to know it wasn't really that hard after all.)

And you know what's even better?

Your words aren't half bad!

Oh, sure, there's some pretty dodgy stuff in there. But if you're honest about it, you've gotta admit, there's some pretty *good* stuff in there, too!

We'll find out for sure soon enough.

Because now that you've got words on the page, you finally get to do what you've been *dying* to do ever since you *started*.

You get to shift gears, and start shredding.

You get to unleash the Movie Critic.

See, you've reached the middle of the FAST System. And that's no small thing.

The midway point is a _major_ transition.

You're not trying to squeeze ideas out of your head anymore. All you need to do now is _fix_ them.

You'll tear your work to pieces, rip it apart, twist it around, hold it upside down, and jiggle the loose coins out of its pockets.

And you'll whip that scrawny little runt into shape.

It'll be a world-class competitor before you know it.

The Objective of this Phase

Last section — the Apply phase — had one purpose. To fill those pages with words. _Any_ words.

Here's why.

You can't _fix_ what isn't broken. You can't _modify_ what's invisible. You can't _improve_ what doesn't exist.

Or, think of it this way: You can't _write_ until you've got words on the page!

Remember the cliché "all writing is _rewriting_"? Well, it might not _literally_ be true, but you can't turn words into a masterpiece until you _have_ some on the page.

Well now you do. Now you've got something to fix.

S is for Strengthen.

And this phase of the FAST System has one purpose, too. To take what you've got, and make it better.

Don't complicate it. That's all this phase is about.

Yes, it can be a little tricky. You've got a million questions. For starters, _how_ do you make it better? How do you even know what you've _got_?

We'll break it down into three "movements."

And each "movement" is a chapter.

First, you'll _inspect_ what you have. See what's there. You can't know what to change until it's clear. That's _this_ chapter.

Second, you'll _decide_ what needs to be done. There are four possibilities. Chapter 11 shows how to make those decisions.

Third, you'll _amplify_ your work. When you know what you've got, and you've decided what to do, all that's left is to _do_ it. Chapter 12 has techniques to get you moving.

In short, we're about to turn your words into gold.

Inspect from a Distance

To *inspect* something is to look at it critically. To hunt for flaws. To examine it. Almost suspiciously.

With your own work, it's easy to be over-critical.

But we don't *want* over-critical. There's no point wasting time with "it's *bad*" or "it's *terrible*."

But then again, we don't want *under*-critical, either. If you think everything you write is brilliant, you'll never improve.

Instead, we want *objectivity*. We need to see what's not working, and figure out how to fix it.

And if you finished getting your words on the page *yesterday*, get outta here. Don't even *try* this today. You couldn't possibly be objective about your work.

You need a break.

How long? I don't know. Maybe a few days. Maybe a couple weeks. Maybe several months.

You need as long as it takes to get *distance* from your words.

Otherwise you'll pay attention to all the wrong things. And instead of writing *fast*, you'll take twice as long.

Imagine you're a football player. You're on the field. In the final minutes of the game, the other team narrowly snatches victory as time runs out.

Would you wander over to the sideline and start immediately reviewing the videotape? Would you pull up a chair and analyze?

Of course not!

You'd do that *later* — off the field! When you're detached from it. When you can look at it with a clear head.

Same goes for your writing.

And it's the same process. But instead of watching videotape, you're watching the replay of your words.

Nothing Personal

The first key to objectivity is to *not* take it personally.

Promise yourself something. When you re-read and analyze your own work, you won't *judge* yourself. You won't cringe. You won't hurl obscenities at yourself.

Because that's not fair. Think about it.

You wrote this thing quickly. And I mean FAST!

Of *course* it has problems. How could it *not*?!

Picture your best friend standing in front of you. He's trying to explain something, but he's stumbling over his words. His sentences are sloppy and grammatically incorrect, and you're not even convinced he *has* a point.

You wouldn't chuck *him* out the window, would you?! (Would you?!) So go easy on yourself. Cut yourself a bit of slack.

The only way to be objective is to forget about "this is good" or "this is terrible."

Instead, use only "this works" or "this doesn't work."

It's reasonable to say, "This chapter isn't very effective." Maybe it has no punch. Or it meanders aimlessly on its way to the point. Or the sentences are repetitious and boring. Or the idea isn't clear. But you can't say, "This chapter sucks."

When you identify *why* your work isn't effective, you're also identifying *how* to turn it around!

And you can't do that if you're busy picking on yourself. So relax. Let's just fix what isn't working.

Feel the Overall Effect

Great. Now that you're detached and objective, it's time to start pulling it to pieces.

To do that, you'll need to read it *twice*.

See, you can't fix the *pieces* until you see the *whole*. So here's the rule for your first read-through:

Read your work. And I mean *read*.

No modifying. No adjusting. No fixing. No correcting. No changing. No Tweaking. No swapping words, or shifting, or blending, or cutting, or pasting, or spelling, or... or *anything!*

You may only read. (You can keep a BIN handy for ideas and notes, but *not* for throwing anything away!)

As you read, feel the overall *effect*. Remember, you're transfering ideas from *your* head to your *reader's* head.

You need to see what you're really transferring!

What's there? What's missing? How is it different to what you expected? Is what you *thought* you were writing what you've actually *written*?

The overall effect is a combination of many things — your

initial ideas, your Focus Plan, your ability to stay on track, your writing style, pace, tone, presentation, and so on.

You'll only get it if you read it, first, *all the way through*.

When you're finished — and *only* when you're finished — write down your impressions. Your thoughts. Ideas that weren't clear. Sections that didn't make sense. What's missing, and what you thought could be stronger.

On your *second* read, you can start making some notes.

The Logic of Your Work

Your brain is a filter.

Think about the last time you were presented with an idea.

You thought about it. You held it up against what you already know about the world. If it seemed reasonable, you let that idea in. If not, you rejected it.

You *filtered* it! You didn't just accept the idea at face value (unless you were sleepy).

And it happened *instantly*.

In fact, you're doing it right now!

As you read through this book, the FAST System is making more and more sense to you — and *as* you see it more clearly, you're either embracing it, or rejecting it.

And it depends on what's already *in* your brain.

If you already write fast, you'll be comparing what *you* do with what I'm suggesting. If it matches, you'll take this on board.

But if this is new to you, you'll be busy imagining how you would apply it. If it makes sense, you'll accept it, right?

Every brain is a logic filter. Yours is filtering *my* writing. Your reader's will filter *your* writing! And that's why logic is so fundamentally important.

If you're writing non-fiction, your case must be clear. Concise. Your *progression* must make sense. The idea must get clearer and more distinct with each page they read.

If it doesn't — if there are any holes along the way — your reader rejects it, and the writing is unsuccessful. (That's when you say ridiculous things like, "It sucks.")

With fiction writing, your story also needs logic and progression. It's known as the "internal consistency" of your story. All stories have to make sense. The reader must understand *why* this scene comes after that one. When a story "builds," it really just means your brain can piece it together effectively.

So as you read your work, watch how it builds.

Have you made any logic mistakes? Is it progressing the way it should? Is the idea becoming clearer? Are there any holes?

Remember, don't get stuck trying to fix it yet. You need to get the overall *effect* of the whole thing, first. Just keep an eye out for the logic and progression of your writing.

Make notes and keep moving. We'll fix it later.

Your Rhythm and Flow

Now, that logic is Left-brained. And it's crucial, if you want to keep your reader reading.

But it's only half of the equation.

The other half is Rhythm and Flow. It's the Right-brain side of your writing. The aesthetic. How it *feels*. How it *flows*.

The "vibe" of the thing.

The flow of your work is what keeps the reader's eyes gliding down the page. Any time the reader stops, or gets stuck, or stumbles over confusing sentences or sections of your writing, you've lost the rhythm. And it happens when the ideas within a section aren't working *together*.

For example, as you were writing, maybe you had a great idea. It should've been thrown in the BIN. But you didn't have anything *else* for that page, so you wrote it. You blasted through.

Well, that's okay while you're speed writing. But as you read it back, it's awkward. Jumbled. It stops the flow (because it was a *stray* idea). The rhythm goes out of step.

It's like the awkward kid on a dance floor. You know *he* hears a rhythm. But it's certainly not what everyone else is listening to. And until they get in sync, it's just embarrassing.

Unfortunately, it's very common. It's easy to break the flow. It happens when you write different parts of a section on different days. Which, let's face it, is *always!*

Each day, your mind is in a slightly different place. (That's why writing has always seemed so difficult!) But you're putting your ideas on the page. They'll be read back *together* — on the *same* day. If they're not consistent, you lose the flow.

Notice it!

See when your writing is spotty, sketchy, jumbled, confusing, awkward or clumsy.

Look for sections or chapters or paragraphs that don't seem to fit. And make a note of it.

Effective writing sets its own rhythm, and everything else flows along in step. Simply. Cleanly.

The ideas should run smoothly from one to the next.

Missing and Redundant Ideas

Now don't forget, we're still only inspecting.

Don't get too carried away trying to find every little thing that's wrong, and every little detail that's out of place. Stay focused on the *ideas* you're getting across. Trying to do it all at once is too much. It's information overload. Keep it simple.

There's only one other thing I want you to look for while you're inspecting. And this one comes naturally:

What's missing, and what's redundant.

Two sides of the same coin.

As you read, the major problems will jump out at you. Whole pieces of your idea will be missing! You raced through this thing, and some ideas you *thought* were there, simply aren't.

Or — and this happened to me continuously as I was writing this book — you discover *new* ideas and new points you didn't originally *know* about your subject when you started. Well, now that you know them, they're missing, too.

On the flip side is redundancy. Ideas that were so important, you repeated them twice. Or three times. Or *twenty*.

This isn't *intentional* repetition, like when I say "all writing is communication." I repeat that to drive home the point.

Instead, "redundancy" is when you get stuck, and repeat yourself because can't think of anything else to say.

It happens for hundreds of reasons: Maybe your Focus Plan wasn't clear enough. Or you wrote on different days (and forgot you wrote it earlier). Or it felt "new" in a different context.

It's natural. And to write *fast*, it's part of the process.

That's *how* you write FAST. You pour it all that onto the page. And when you get *here*, you notice it. And then you make notes. You identify it. And then you keep moving.

As long as you see it, you're ready to make your list.

Your Problem List

Imagine you're taking an old car in for a check-up. What happens? The mechanic inspects it for problems.

First is the once-over. Overall, it looks okay. But then we go in for a closer look. No, the headlight's busted. There's rust on the back passenger door. The engine has a rattle sound.

And the mechanic scribbles every problem onto a sheet of paper. When he's done, he's got a list of everything that's wrong with your car.

That's what we're doing with your writing.

You've been through the inspection, now. It's time to draw up the report.

And before you think of skipping this step, remember. You want to write *fast*, right? Which would you prefer? A mechanic who works from a Problem List? Or one who just starts pulling apart your engine and fiddling as he goes?

Your Problem List is organized however you like.

It's a list of what's wrong. Not the *words*. But the overview.

The *ideas*, the logic, the progression, the holes, the flow, the rhythm, and whatever is missing or redundant.

Big picture stuff.

Break your writing into sections. Start with a list of project problems. Then zoom in. Create a list of major section problems (for this book, I might have a problem list for each of the six sections). Then zoom in. Create a list of chapter problems. And then segment problems. Down to the smallest thought.

You'll love this part. It's what you've been waiting for!

And it's crucial for two reasons.

Firstly, it's therapeutic. When you physically *list* everything that's wrong with your project, you detach from it.

And secondly, you get your mind thinking in "revision mode." It's not about "writing" anymore. It's about *fixing*.

And it's only effective after *two* reads of your work. The first gives you a sense of it. The second gets specific.

Just remember. No editing, rewriting, tweaking or adjusting.

Ideas and overview *only*. Just make a Problem List.

And then in the next chapter, we'll decide what to do about all those problems.

Inspect Your Work in 5 Easy Steps

Writers often get lost when they see a mountain of pages they've written. But not you. Never again. Just follow these five easy steps to see what you've got.

1. <u>**Put yourself in the reader's shoes**</u>.
   You think your work is terrible. Doesn't matter. You're not the important one here. Your reader is. Take time off if you need to, but *detach* from your work. When you can look at your work objectively, then:

2. <u>**Read it through completely**</u>.
   No red pencil yet. If you get a great *idea*, jot it down (no need to lose those slippery beasts), but do *not* fix your work on the first read. Just get a sense of it. Feel the whole. Then:

3. <u>**Write down your thoughts**</u>.
   At the end of the first read, write down your impressions. Your overall feelings. The big picture. The point is to see how far off you are from expressing your idea. Take as much time as you need, and then:

4. <u>**Re-read and make notes**</u>.
   On your *second* read of the material, use the red pencil. Get aggressive. Note everything that isn't working (and *why* it's not working, if you can tell). No fixing yet. Just mark up your text. Be detailed. Then:

5. <u>**Create your Problem List**</u>.
   Assemble all your notes into a list. Major section problems first. Then zoom in to each level, and create a list of problems for each one.

You'll end up with a list of what's not working. There's no "good" or "bad" here. Look for the *effectiveness* of your words, instead. Make notes of everything you need to fix.

There's no timeframe for it. It could take twenty minutes, twenty days, or twenty weeks. But don't take too long. Inspect *fast*. You can always come back and do it again.

And so...

After all that ranting and raving about how terrible you think your work is, it's very weird to get to this phase and suddenly have to pull your work to pieces.

You'll find that things aren't so bad after all, in some spots. (And other areas make you want to hide under the nearest rock.)

Be strong. Be brutal. Be honest.

But don't be unfair.

It's not a question of whether your work is "good" or not. Some of it's good, some of it isn't. That's true of all writing. The words you're reading right now — my words — some of it's good, and some of it isn't.

Doesn't matter.

The question is how *effective* is it? How *clear* is it?

Ask yourself whether it *works* or not. Whether it gets your idea across in the best possible way.

In the next chapter, we'll put your Problem List to good use.

And you'll finally — *finally* — have a way of fixing all that rubbish that just spilled out of you.

Not a bad deal, dontcha think?

So.

Feeling like a writer yet?

11

Decide Which Way to Go

You're about to make some big decisions.

And if you're anything like me, decisions are trauma.

So forgive me if I get a little philosophical for a minute (hey, why stop now, right?), but I've learned a life lesson over the past few years. And I want to share it with you.

Before I held my first screenwriting workshops, I had never sold a screenplay. I'd been writing (off and on) for about fifteen years, but I didn't even consider myself a writer.

I had written a feature-length screenplay that a friend and I co-produced ourselves. And I had seen that project from the first spark of the idea, all the way through post-production and marketing. So I planned to teach from the *producer's* perspective.

But I'd never taught screenwriting before. And I didn't have a name anybody knew. And... and I got scared.

No. Not scared. *Terrified!*

In the lead-up to those first workshops, I freaked out. What if they hated me? What if I choked? What if I got run out of town? I would be standing in front of fourteen people for a whole weekend. Being watched. Inspected. Judged.

What if I was terrible?

The fear began to consume me.

I was literally *this close* to canceling it and refunding the deposits I had taken. And I faced a decision: Run the workshops, or run and hide!

When, suddenly, a simple little thought popped into my head.

"What if they love it?"

I had gotten so carried away with the fear of what could go *wrong* that I forgot to look at what could go *right*.

So I decided to *do* the workshops — even if I *did* fail. If I failed, at least I'd learn something.

(And it's the same thought that pushes me through this book.)

It's funny. Not only did I rise to the challenge, but the workshops were an enormous success. The participants gave me overwhelmingly positive feedback (it totally blew me away). And — and this is the kicker — those workshops led directly to opportunities with three other film producers. Opportunities I would never have come across if I had chickened out.

Ideas spark ideas.

So here's the lesson: When you face a choice you're unsure about, *just decide*. Jump in with both feet, and keep moving forward. Be bold! Put yourself out there, and doors you've never seen will open. You never saw them because you didn't know they existed. But they do. And they're yours for the taking.

You can quote me on this:

Life will give you everything you ever want.

All it asks in return is a little show of bravery.

The Big Decisions

Every problem you've identified in your Problem List represents a decision you have to make. Should it stay? Should it go? Should it get enhanced, reduced, modified, twisted, adjusted, spun around, turned inside out? All of the above?!

So now that you've got a detailed Problem List, you're left scratching your head.

How do you know which way is right? How do you know what to do? And from all the possible choices, how do you *decide*?

The answer? You keep it simple:

You compare the writing on the page to the *idea* in your head.

Now that you've pulled apart your writing and made notes and lists of problems, you're a little more objective about it. (Notice I said a *little* more...)

You didn't fix anything, because we're not there yet. And this is where so many writers go wrong. You start fixing as soon as you notice something's wrong, and then you get lost in the middle of the rewrite.

And I *know* you do it. Because I do it, too!

Truth be told, this book was delayed — for *exactly* that reason! Even though I *knew* not to do it, I did it anyway. Listen, we've gotta be vigilant about this. If you want to write *fast*, you've got break your work into systematic pieces.

Inspect. Decide. Amplify. Break it up.

You can't *decide* which way to go when you're in the middle of pushing in another direction.

You can only decide by looking at the problems objectively.

And the way to do that, is to grade your work.

Grade Your Writing

Don't worry. This has nothing to do with school. It's not a "grade" like "A+" or "F". It's more like the grade of a ski slope. "Double black diamond" might be a steep cliff. "Double green circle" might be a bunny hill that's virtually *flat*.

At this stage, every chunk of your writing will fit into one of four categories. And the categories have nothing to do with how "good" it is. Instead, they grade how "effective" it is.

And we'll *use* the grades to make it *more* effective.

The grades are: *Re-Focus*, *Research*, *Edit* or *Tweak*.

Re-Focus means the section (chapter/segment/etc.) misses the mark entirely. It needs a major re-think. When you Re-Focus, you'll send that chunk through the Focus *and* Apply phases again.

Research means the idea is there, but it's not very effective, detailed, or authentic. It needs a whole new layer of... well... *something*. You'll get that "something" through research.

Edit means the idea is there, and it's effective, but it's awkward and clunky, and doesn't work in the context of your project. You'll need to blend and cut and re-shape.

And *Tweak* means the underlying ideas and presentation are pretty solid. The *words* might need a lot of work — it might need a lot more *zing* — but the *idea* is ready for the next phase.

Different sections may go through *each* of these grades before they're ready. And that's perfectly okay. (It won't take as long as you might suspect, either.)

The grades give us a way of determining where we are, and

where we need to go. By grading your work, you'll map out your rewrite effortlessly. You'll have a map that shows you exactly which way to go.

But how do we determine which grades to give? How can you tell which way to take your writing? How do you know what "works" and what doesn't?

The Stack Test

It took me awhile to figure this one out. And, like all efficient solutions (including the FAST System itself), once it hit me, it seemed so painfully obvious.

I call it the Stack Test, and it's remarkably simple.

All writing is communication.

All communication is the transfer of ideas.

Your job is to put *your* idea into your *reader's* head.

And to do that, your writing needs to build logically in its own natural progression.

Do we agree on that so far? (Please say yes.)

The Stack Test, then, simply looks at everything you write, and asks whether this section/segment/chapter/act/paragraph/sentence/whatever *stacks on top of* what you've previously built.

Imagine the *idea* is a brick wall. Each section is a brick.

Does this brick stack on top of the one before it, or not?

For example, as you read this book, you get to each chapter and feel like you "get it." You have a better and better sense of what the FAST System is all about, right?

But then (if I'm doing my job right), you get *into* the chapter — into the *meat* of it — and discover a new piece of the puzzle. And when you do, the idea becomes even clearer. Right?

That's because the *book* is about a *whole* idea.

But each chapter *within* the book is there to *build* that idea. If I spent a whole chapter on my visit to the Grand Canyon last year, it wouldn't fit. It might be entertaining (ask me about it sometime), but it doesn't build the idea of this book.

So it's gotta go. (Re-Focus.)

Or be made relevant. (Research.)

Or blended in somewhere else. (Edit.)

Until it's organic to the whole book. (Tweak.)

Make sense?

When to Re-Focus

On a day when you're feeling a lot of self-loathing and pity, you'll want to put *everything* in the Re-Focus category.

Don't.

If you actually *did* go through the Focus phase, you shouldn't need to Re-Focus as much as you think. (If you jumped into it — like I did — this is where you learn never to do *that* again.)

Only Re-Focus when your writing is *completely* muddled. And I mean completely. You tried. Really, you did. But it just ain't working. You need to try something else.

You need a whole new brick.

How does it happen? How can you go so far off track?

There are a million reasons. You tried to make it tangible, but *this* approach didn't work. Or you came up with *better* ideas as you wrote. Or stray tangents kept interrupting (and you didn't put them in your BIN). Or as you look at it now, your writing doesn't fit the format (novel, screenplay, article, whatever).

Whatever the reason, only chuck out what genuinely needs to be Re-Focused.

Avoid re-starting the whole project from scratch.

If you keep "starting over" every time you write something, you'll be spinning your wheels and getting nowhere.

Here's the rule of thumb.

Don't Re-Focus until you know *exactly how* you're going to do it. Take the time to figure out your new approach. And don't delete the original writing. (Just in case it looks better later.)

In other words, don't just toss things out because you're grumpy. When you Re-Focus a section, you're starting that section from scratch, to make your idea stronger.

Always Re-Focus to Strengthen — never to avoid.

When to Research

A few hundred years ago, when explorers ventured out into the world, they would come back with magnificent exaggerated tales of giants, and natives, and secret villages, and such.

And readers believed every word. They *had* to. Who's gonna question it? They had no way of knowing any different!

Today, forget about it. The internet changed the world. Information is at your fingertips. Heck, the whole *world* is at your fingertips. If you start telling magnificent exaggerated tales, you'll get lambasted.

But it's even more subtle than that.

If you don't know your topic, your reader will *know* you don't know it. Darabont couldn't write *Shawshank* without researching prisons of that era.

If I wanted to write a scene about two lovers scuba diving in the Bahamas, I'd better do a little research. Either that, or pray my readers live in a room with no windows and no phone lines.

Give your work a Research grade when it's got holes. When you *like* the basic idea and the *way* you're presenting it. But it needs *more*. It needs to be authentic.

Research brings your work to life, and gives it a new layer of energy, and realism. Learn! Discover more about this idea you're writing about. You'll find new ways to write about it.

The trouble is, these new details will change your writing. It'll shift. They'll make you adjust other parts, too. And that's why Research is the second "strongest" grade.

With a Re-Focus grade, you'll find a new approach.

With a Research grade, you'll keep the idea, but change its *substance*.

Give a section a Research grade when the Apply phase has pushed you too quickly through it — and you want to go deeper.

When to Edit

Editing is a broad topic.

Editing means revising, changing and fixing your work.

Technically, the Strengthen and Tweak phases are both "editing." Editing has typically meant the whole rewriting process.

But to my way of thinking, that definition is too broad.

Editing should be specific. It's rearranging, blending, and cutting what you've got. It's not rewriting. It's not tweaking.

I like to keep every movement separate. Systematic.

Your project is like a jigsaw puzzle, with extra pieces from another box. You've got to determine the best fit of the pieces, and get rid of stray pieces that don't belong.

Give an Edit grade when the *idea* is there, and the *detail* is rich enough, but the pieces aren't fitting correctly. It's choppy or jumbled or in need of rearranging.

For example, when I write, I always *over*write. I ramble on and on, and say way too much. If I'm writing a 10-page chapter, I'll write 15 pages, knowing I'll chop them down later.

But I end up with a lot of material I don't need. Or stories that may or may not fit. All the way through! Cutting a section *here* affects other sections over *there*. So I'll go through and Edit everything, to give the whole piece the right flow and tone.

Give your work the Edit grade when your idea is clear and your detail is solid, but the writing itself needs to be rearranged, cut, blended, and organized.

When to Tweak

We'll get into Tweaking in more detail in the next section, so I'll keep this brief.

Give your writing a Tweak grade when the idea is clear, the detail is solid, and it's arranged pretty much how you want it to be arranged.

In other words, when your work is passing the Stack Test.

Tweaking is the process of going through your work, and steering the reader's eyeballs. Making sure your writing has the exact effect you want it to have.

We'll get into *how* to do that starting with Chapter 13.

For now, just remember that the Tweak *grade* means that section is ready for the Tweak *phase*.

And you're not done with the Strengthen phase until you give *every* section a Tweak grade. And you'll go through each of the other grades to get there.

Create a Strengthen Plan

Now here's where you bring it all together. Time to prioritize.

When you have your work marked up, and you've graded each chunk, it's time to put it into a plan.

Just as the *Focus Plan* prepared you for writing, the *Strengthen Plan* prepares you for rewriting.

Here's how to put it together:

On a sheet of paper, or a new file on the computer, create a *line* for each element of your writing — however you've broken it down (Acts, chapters, scenes, sections, chunks, whatever).

On each line, list the section, the grade you gave it, and the time you estimate it'll take to finish it. For example:

"Create a Strengthen Plan" — Edit — 20 minutes.
"Decide in 5 Easy Steps" — Re-Focus — 3 hours.
"And so..." — Tweak

(If anything gets a *Tweak* grade, don't give it a time. It's ready for the next phase!)

Go through your Problem List. Create a line for every section, every sub-section, every chunk. Do it for *every level*.

Then, arrange each line in order of priority.

All sections with a *Re-Focus* grade go together. All *Research* sections go together. All *Edit* sections go together.

The only exception is that the *level* always gets top priority. The *grade* comes second.

In other words, "Chapter 11" would get priority over "5 Easy Steps" — even if it has a lower grade — because "Chapter 11" is the higher level.

For example, let's say "Chapter 11" gets a *Research* grade, but "5 Easy Steps" gets a *Re-Focus* grade. It's pointless fixing smaller sections first — they might get cut later!

So you'd arrange it like so:

Chapter 11 — Research – 6 hours
   "5 Easy Steps" — Re-Focus — 3 hours
   "Create a Strengthen Plan" — Edit — 20 minutes
   "And so..." — Tweak

What you're doing is creating an *order* for your rewrite. You're giving yourself a way to simplify it. So you'll *do* it!

Go through your notes, estimate times, and prioritize. If you don't know how much time to estimate, just guess. As a guide, use the time it took you to get through the Focus and Apply phases. Estimating takes practice. You'll get faster with experience.

And when you've finished turning your Problem List into a Strengthen Plan, guess what?

You've got a custom roadmap to fix your work. Nifty, huh?

Decide Which Way to Go in 5 Easy Steps

In this part of the Strengthen phase, you're planning the rewrite. If you don't plan ahead, it's easy to get lost in a sea of pages. Here's how to do it in five easy steps.

1. Review your Problem List.
   See what you've got, and where it needs fixing. Trust your instincts. Look at the project as a *whole*, and then zoom in to each section, down to each chunk, as you:

2. Apply the Stack Test.
   Be honest. Is your idea building? If not — or if the flow isn't right — where does it go off the rails? The Stack Test applies to *every* level of your writing, even down to individual sentences. But for now, watch the overview — how your idea builds. And, *as* you're applying the Stack Test:

3. Grade each element.
   Next to each element (section/chapter/page/scene/whatever) on your Problem List, give it a grade. Everything is either *Re-Focus*, *Research*, *Edit*, or *Tweak*. In that order. Don't be too harsh, but don't go too easy, either. When every element has a grade, then:

4. Prioritize the results.
   Arrange the elements in order of priority. All *Re-Focus* elements in one group, all *Research* elements in another, etc. Major sections (e.g., chapters) get priority over smaller elements (e.g. scenes). When you're done, then:

5. Create your Strengthen Plan.
   You've identified the problems. You've graded everything. You've prioritized. Now give each element an estimated time, and map out your plan to *do* it. It's your roadmap for the rewrite. A step-by-step list of which section needs what, and the order in which to do them.

In this step, we separate the forest from the trees, and create the plan of action. This is *not* as hard as it seems. Go through it quickly. Trust your instincts, and keep moving.

And so...

The trouble with writing is that there are so many choices available to you, it's impossible to know which one is "right."

When you get into the middle of it, the problem multiplies. The ideas are bouncing around in your head like never before! And there are so many *good* ideas! (And so many stinkers, too.)

It's incredibly easy to get lost.

So here's a rule:

Don't over-think this!

Go with your gut reactions! Look at your Problem List, read the section, consider how effective it is, give it a grade, move on. Do it quickly. Instinctively.

You can always come back later. If you Re-Focus something, and then grade the new version and it *still* gets a Re-Focus grade, you'll do it again anyway! So relax.

Remember, you're *not* fixing it yet! There's no pressure.

All you're doing is grading your work and creating a plan.

By doing this, you're telling yourself that it's *doable*, that you can fix it systematically, and that each side of your brain gets a chance to help out.

Making decisions about your own work is one of the hardest things for writers. You either want to cut everything, or you want to *keep* everything.

Always remember that *there is no right or wrong*. And the decisions you make are based on your opinion.

It's your work, and *you* have the final say.

Don't make decisions out of insecurity *or* over-confidence. Make every decision according to how *effective* that piece of writing is — how well it expresses or builds the idea.

And when you finish, every element of your writing will have a grade. And you'll know exactly what you need to do.

You'll be ready for the rewrite.

Interesting, huh?

This writing thing is looking pretty doable after all.

12 Amplify for Maximum Effect

Alright, here we go.

This is where you turn your words into gold.

But before we get started, I want to make something perfectly clear. Everybody hates this part. It's where writers get stuck. They go over their work, again and again, and lose all sight of the forest. The trees keep jumping out and sucker-punching them.

You can spend an ungodly amount of time thrashing your arms about in this section. And if you aren't careful, you *will*.

The trick is to take it one step at a time. And keep moving.

Listen, writing is subjective. Keep reminding yourself. I'll repeat, in case there's any confusion: *Writing is subjective!* There is no "good" or "bad." There is no "right" or "wrong."

There's only *clear* or *unclear* — *effective* or *ineffective*.

And even *that* comes in varying degrees.

If you don't take this to heart — truly take it on board — you will swim in this chapter for the rest of your natural born life.

And it's not even my favorite chapter.

So I don't want that to happen.

This chapter is *not* about "101 ways to Strengthen your writing." Each format (novel, screenplay, term paper, business plan, whatever) is different. They each have their own requirements.

No. Instead, this chapter is about the *approach* to your rewrite. It's about the *system* that will push you through it.

It's about "amplifying" your work, *in general*. And you'll only get through it *one* way. By taking it one step at a time.

One Step at a Time

To "amplify" your writing is to make your ideas clearer. Stronger. More effective.

And the process is unbelievably simple (even though I *know* you want to complicate it).

All you have to do is fix what you've got.

That's all. That's it!

Yes, I *know* it's "easier said than done." But don't lose sight of it. Simple is *always* better. Don't over-complicate it, or you'll get stuck. In fact, over-complicating it is *why* you get stuck!

Look, you're not striving for perfection yet. We'll do that in the Tweak phase. For now, you're just amplifying. Turning it up a notch, and making it work. Getting it ready to be Tweaked.

And you've already done two-thirds of the work.

You inspected your writing. Graded it. And you've got a Problem List, and a Strengthen Plan.

Now, you simply blast through each element (chapter, chunk, section, whatever), and get it to the next grade.

Turn a *Re-Focus* chunk into a *Research* chunk.

Turn a *Research* into an *Edit*.

Turn an *Edit* into a *Tweak*.

If you accidentally turn a *Re-Focus* into a *Tweak*, fantastic! But don't expect it. Don't even *strive* for that. Just go from one grade to the next. Easy does it. You'll actually go faster that way.

Re-writing is only difficult when you look at it the wrong way. You probably think you need to "create" all over again. From scratch.

But you don't. All you're doing in this stage is *fixing* what's there. Making it better. Amplifying it.

Re-writing is as simple or as difficult as you make it. Blast through it as quickly as you blasted through the Apply phase.

And I mean FAST! Okay?

The Stages of Revision

The first secret to rewriting is this: Take it in stages. Don't try to make it perfect from the very start. It's too big to do all at once. By taking it in stages, you make it manageable.

Let's look at the stages:

Re-Focus. This is your least effective writing.

In your Strengthen Plan, every section with a Re-Focus grade goes back to the start of the FAST System — back to F, for Focus. Figure out your idea, and make it tangible. Break it into chunks. And then speed write it again. Let go. See where it takes you. Do these sections first.

Research. This is writing that needs to improve.

This is where you start controlling the outcome. Everything with a Research grade needs more detail. Learn more about your topic. Fill in your missing knowledge. Use what you learn to shape your writing, strengthen your ideas, and more effectively express your idea. Research when all Re-Focusing is done.

Edit. This is writing that needs to be massaged into place.

Like a master engineer, move the pieces around to snap the puzzle together. Shift, cut, blend and rework it. This is a very deliberate stage — take charge of your writing. Control it. Steer it. Until now, your writing has taken *you* for the ride. Now *you* reclaim command. Edit when there's nothing left to Research.

Tweak. You won't touch this writing until the next phase.

This is where you perfect it — where you control the flow of your *words* to give it exactly the right effect. This comes *last. Do not tweak during the rewrite!* Once you've given everything a Tweak grade, you're done Strengthening. Congratulations.

As you go through your Strengthen Plan, take these stages in this order. It helps keep you focused. If you improve each of the *Re-Focus* sections first, and bump their grades up to *Research*, your project is at a new level. It's better. It's stronger. And you'll *feel* that difference. You'll feed off it.

After you rewrite each section, grade it again. If you decide it's *still* the same grade, do it again. Quickly. Keep pushing.

Only *you* know when the idea is right. Each time you go through *each* of these stages, you'll get closer to that idea.

And figuring out what *doesn't* work is just as valuable as figuring out what *does*.

Control the Outcome

It's *essential* to divide your rewrite into these stages. If you jump around, you'll get lost in the abyss of rewriting.

Take this to heart: Rewriting can take forever — but only if you want it to. Maybe you want it to. If so, have *fun* with it! But if you want to get *through* it, there's no need for that.

Instead, push through. Don't get stuck. Express your idea as effectively as possible, and then move on, and forget about it.

Your Strengthen Plan is your guide.

Go through it step by step. Inch by inch. Break it down into chunks, just like you did for your Focus Plan. The Focus Plan used blocks of *pages* to help you through it. The Strengthen Plan uses blocks of *time*.

Grab hold of it. Steer it. Forget perfection. Just dig in.

Look, when you've got a whole bunch of blank pages staring at you, you need to let yourself go, and let the words pour out of you onto the page.

But once they're *on* the page, you've got to steer them. Shape them. Craft them. You've got to deliberately put them in the order that amplifies their effect, and strikes that bolt of lightning.

And you can. Don't let those words intimidate you. Any (and *every*) word you've written can be thrown out entirely. Or it can be adjusted and strenghtened. It's up to you. Take charge!

But move quickly. And keep going.

By now, your *idea* should be pretty clear. Even if it wasn't clear when you started, just by writing all those words and pushing through this process, your idea will have revealed itself.

Control this beast. Tame it. It's yours.

Clarity and Impact

To put your idea into someone else's mind, that idea needs to be clear and direct. And have just the right impact.

When you graded your Problem List, you instinctively spotted clarity and impact problems. The steeper the grade (Re-Focus and Research), the less clarity and impact.

Now, as you rewrite, make it clear. Get your meaning across. Avoid confusion. Hunt for things that might be misunderstood.

And don't lose sight of where you're going.

In writing, everything is connected. Every idea, every *word*, puts an idea in your reader's head. If *every* word isn't working together, that idea gets confused. Jumbled. Garbled.

For example, as I'm Strengthening this book, I'm struggling. The reason is this: Every time I read back a chapter, I see a different level of it. The "overview" might work fine. But the segment goes off on a tangent.

But then the *next* time I read the chapter back, I have the opposite feeling. The "overview" feels disjointed to me. But the segment works fine on its own.

What's going on here?!

You're trying to juggle each of the levels in your head at the same time. Stop it! Focus on one at a time.

Keep it simple.

During the *Re-Focus* stage, focus on creating a new approach that simplifies your idea. Don't be clever. Be *clearer*. Look for a new approach that clarifies your idea.

Then, during the *Research* stage, explore what you've written. Look for new details and depth to pinpoint your idea. As you research, find specifics that nail it. Specifics that make it clear and give it extra punch.

And then during the *Edit* stage, look for ways to chop and shift and rearrange to heighten that impact. Always making the idea clear. Always serving the underlying idea of your project.

Be active. Consciously watch (and fix!) the clarity and impact of your writing. If you do, you won't get stuck.

Cutting, Blending, and Rearranging

Now, particularly when you get to the *Edit* stage, the work of rewriting involves mostly cutting, blending and rearranging.

Right here, for example.

I just cut out three paragraphs.

Why? Because I've got a better way to communicate the idea. And I think this *new* way will be clearer for you, and have a greater impact.

See, originally, I had each idea — cutting, blending, and rearranging — as its own paragraph. Separated.

But no, they're *not* separate. At least not the way I want you to think of them.

Instead, think of them as a trio. Cutting, blending, and rearranging. Like Larry, Moe and Curly (or Shemp, if you prefer).

If your idea is unclear (or redundant, or confusing, or it's got no impact), whip out the trio, and start fiddling.

Cutting is when you get rid of something (obviously). But as soon as you do it, you need to blend what came before and after. And you'll rearrange to keep the flow smooth.

Don't let your reader thump over a gaping pothole. Cut, blend and rearrange paragraphs, segments, or even whole chapters to keep the idea building. This is how you amplify for effect.

And the reader won't even see it.

Just like you didn't see what I did there.

Well. Unless you realize I just told you. Hmm. Get it?

Fix and Move On

Now, do you remember how quickly you went through the Apply phase? Notice how *speed* made the whole process easier.

Well, in this phase, you're letting the Movie Critic out, and allowing him to point out the flaws in your work.

You've got to keep that guy on a short leash.

He can make a criticism, but as soon as you fix it, he's not allowed to say any more.

Not until you come back later.

For example, let's say you read a segment of a chapter you've written, and the voice in your head says it's clumsy and wordy, and the idea isn't clear. You need to *Edit* it.

Cool. No problem. You take out three paragraphs here, slide two up from the bottom, rewrite the next one, and then add two new paragraphs at the end. Then you read it back over.

Here's the important part.

If it's *close*, move on.

Forget making it perfect. And this is absolutely 100% *vital* if you're writing long-form (novels, books, screenplays, etc). If it's close, move on!

Don't dwell on it. Don't keep spinning your wheels. Nobody knows the *order* you wrote each chapter! Heck, you could even start at the end and work your way back to the beginning!

Your reader would never know.

So go FAST. The faster you fix, the easier fixing will be.

That's not permission to be sloppy. Be honest when you grade. If it isn't clear, don't grade higher because you're bored.

But don't go around in circles, either.

As you fix it and move on, you'll gradually push each chunk through each stage of revision. And if you follow this system, you'll be done faster than you ever thought possible.

If you're already *applying* this book, you can see it for yourself. (I'm seeing it with my own writing, so I know it's effective!)

If you're still just reading, get started soon.

And then you'll be nearly finished by now.

Objective Feedback

Rewriting your own work is a complex job. But by moving through your Strengthen Plan one step at a time, focusing on your *idea* instead of the words, you can do it.

And, I believe, you *must*.

It's important to always Strengthen your own work first.

For two reasons.

Firstly, you're the only one that knows what you're trying to say. It's *your* idea. I can't say it for you. Nobody else can either.

And secondly, the more you do it, the better you'll get. Soon, you'll be able to grade, prioritize and fix ideas *automatically* as you're writing them (in the Apply phase).

But after you've been working on it awhile, you'll start to lose objectivity. You just know too much. You *always* understand your idea better than anyone else. And that makes it easy to miss something — to *think* something is clear when it really isn't.

When that happens, you need objective feedback. A fresh pair of eyes. (I even released a Limited Edition version of this book — because I couldn't see it objectively anymore!)

But be careful here.

Everyone's got an opinion, and most are different to yours. So get your work as good as *you* can make it, first — get everything to the Tweak grade — *before* you solicit feedback.

And evaluate the feedback carefully. It doesn't matter if they think it's "good" or not. What you need to know is if your idea is coming across the way you want it to. What do they think it's about? What does it mean? Get their reaction to your *ideas*.

Now, some kinds of writing will need a *professional* opinion. For example, I know a lot about screenwriting, and I can tell you this: Never let your family or friends judge your screenplay. Screenwriting has such specific requirements, that if they don't know the finer points, their well-meaning opinions can *hurt* you instead of help.

But only get professional help *after* you've made it the very best you can.

You may want to wait until after you've Tweaked your work, but it depends on what you've got, and what you're writing.

Just remember, you're writing for a *reader*. The best way to get a truly objective opinion, is by showing it to one.

Strengthen on 20 Minutes a Day

As I began to rewrite this book, it took longer than I expected. The trouble was, I couldn't hold the ideas *as* I rewrote.

For example, I'd read this chapter, and I'd see what needed to be fixed. I'd write down the Problems, and then create the plan to fix them.

But when I started fixing, ideas sparked ideas, and I'd quickly get lost. What point was I trying to make? What was my original impression of this chapter? How did I plan to fix it, again?

Just *reading* a chapter back would take half an hour. And the more work it needed, the easier it was to get overwhelmed.

My solution?

Do it in highly-focused 20-minute blocks.

Strengthen on 20-minutes a day.

Keep your BIN handy for stray ideas, and charge through your rewrites. For example, if I needed to *Re-Focus* a whole chapter, I'd sketch over it, sprinkling new ideas and detail into each section. I'd outline it in one furious 20-minute block.

Then I'd go back and spend 20 minutes on a segment. Then 20 minutes on the next. And so on.

It worked like a charm.

And as I thought about it, it made sense.

The entire FAST System is about taking this overwhelmingly complex job — writing — and breaking it down into bite-sized chunks. And then just doing one chunk at a time.

Rewrite in the same way. One... step... at... a... time.

Amplify your Writing in 5 Easy Steps

Now that you know *how* to improve your work, it's time to *do* it. Blast through with these five easy steps.

1. <u>Prepare to work quickly</u>.
   The faster you cycle through the rewrites, the better. Don't spend days on the same chunk. Move through them quickly, and come back to them later. Ideas spark ideas, and your Factory's got plenty of them. First up, you'll:

2. <u>Re-Focus for clarity</u>.
   Anything that got a *Re-Focus* grade goes back through the Focus & Apply phases again. Exactly as you did before. When you're done, grade it again. Repeat this as often as necessary, until the grade improves. When it does, then:

3. <u>Research for detail</u>.
   Take anything that got a *Research* grade, and learn more about it. Go to the library, the internet, or whatever source is appropriate. Shape your work with these new discoveries. Rewrite, re-read, and grade again. If it doesn't improve, research more. If it does, then:

4. <u>Edit for impact</u>.
   Take anything that has an *Edit* grade (should be all but the Tweak chunks now), and cut, blend and rearrange. Go for maximum effectiveness. When you're done, grade it again. Repeat the cycle until each element effectively builds your idea. And always remember:

5. <u>One notch at a time</u>.
   Don't try to jump from *Re-Focus* to *Tweak*. Easy does it. Every time you repeat a cycle, you get closer to your idea. Improve in small doses, and keep pushing forward.

Rewriting is simple. You have the ideas, and the solutions are inside you. Let them out. Don't try for perfection — that's the Tweak phase. For now, just make your *ideas* clearer.

Work quickly, fix, and move on. It's better to repeat each each cycle than to get stuck on any single element.

And so...

The Strengthen Phase can be the most challenging phase of the entire writing process. And the reason is simple. You can't see the forest for the trees. You're swimming around in the *detail*, and you lose sight of the *idea* you're trying to get across.

This section simplifies that process.

And here's a quick recap, to make it perfectly clear.

When you've got pages full of your writing (a manuscript, a first-draft screenplay, a rough draft of your thesis, whatever), you've got something to work with.

Go through it, and create a Problem List (Chapter 10). You're trying to see what you've got, and what needs to be fixed. You need to see it clearly before you can do anything with it.

Then, go through it again. This time, grade it, prioritize it and create a Strengthen Plan (Chapter 11). You're turning the Problems into solutions, and giving yourself a roadmap.

Then, simply go through each section in order of priority, and rework, fix, and rewrite until *every* section has a Tweak grade (Chapter 12).

Do it FAST. Don't dwell on it, and don't demand perfection. We'll tweak it later (in the next section). For now, just get your ideas across. Clearly. And with impact.

Shape the lightning bolts on the page.

Building them as you go.

It's a systematic approach. And if you apply it, you *won't get lost!* The reason writers get lost at this stage, is they aren't holding everything up to the *idea* they're trying to express.

And now that you *do*, you can make your work sparkle in no time at all.

[TWEAK]

Turn Your Gold Into Speed

66 The difference between the right word
and almost the right word
is the difference between lightning
and the lightning bug. **99**

—Mark Twain

13 Sharpen the Speed of the Read

The irony of the FAST System is that it doesn't start to come together until the very end. It's a puzzle, whose true power can only be seen when the final piece snaps into place.

Here. In the Tweak Phase.

Over the next three chapters, you'll get a ton of helpful, useful, practical information. And you're gonna have *one* thought, the whole time:

Why didn't you say this stuff sooner?!

Here's why.

If you want to write *fast*, you cannot think. You cannot let your head get in the way. And the tools in this section are thinking tools. I don't want you to use them until *after* your work is on the page.

(Unfortunately, I know how you are. You'll read this before you ever actually *apply* it — despite my pleading. So just pretend you've done all the work the whole way through. If you can see these chapters as if you *had* just experienced the FAST System, you just might glimpse its power.)

So I'll assume you've finished Strengthening your project.

And if you have — seriously — how amazing has the journey been?! You've astounded yourself! You never thought you'd write so much so quickly. You never thought you could *let go* like you have.

You've seen the raw power of writing at lightning speed.

Now, let's let your *reader* tap into that same power.

The Objective of this Phase

If all writing is communication, and communication is the transfer of an idea from your head into the reader's head, then it stands to reason that *putting* the idea into the reader's head is the writer's most important task.

There's a problem, though. No reader's gonna let you put your idea into their head unless they think you've got something valuable for them. Readers are suspicious. Readers are busy. Readers don't have time for us.

So we've got to keep them interested. We've got to get inside their Idea Factory.

And there's only one way in. Through the main entrance. Those grand double doors: the reader's eyeballs.

To transfer your idea into your reader's mind, you need to *control* those eyeballs. And that's what this stage is all about.

T is for Tweak.

The Tweak phase is where you drive the reader's eyes down your page, gobbling up your idea as they go.

Good writing *reads* fast. Ultimately, it doesn't really matter how fast you wrote it. All that matters is how well it reads. If it ain't compelling, the idea won't stick.

In this section, we'll charge your writing with energy. We'll see how to take what you've got, and juice it up, to keep your reader hanging on every word.

Think about the lightning bolt. That crack of the thunder as each new idea claps inside your mind. And when it does, you buzz with electricity.

Now, let's take that image one step further.

Like a brooding storm, those bolts of lightning — your ideas — are raging around inside your head. You want your reader to grasp those ideas, right? How do you do that? Simple.

Get those bolts of lightning to *leap* off the page, and strike your reader in the eyes! Imagine a flash of energy zapping out of the words on the page, and shooting directly into your reader's pupils! They go in through the double-doors and kick off a lightning storm inside your reader's Idea Factory!

Ideas spark ideas.

Take you and me, right now. Our minds are connected.

Right now, my lightning bolts are firing! I'm buzzing with electricity. And I pour these words onto the page.

As you read them, the sparks from my mind touch off the lightning bolts inside your own mind. And if you see what I see — if my picture is clear to you — you start buzzing, too!

That's the power of the picture.

Can you see how a vivid image can transfer an idea?

That's what we'll do with *your* writing in the Tweak phase.

The Philosophy of Tweak

The first time you apply the FAST System, you'll struggle to see the difference between "editing" and "tweaking." (And yes, even though I'm pointing it out, you'll *still* struggle to see the difference.)

The key difference is this: When you edit, you're working on the idea. When you tweak, you're working on the words.

I've made this distinction to *separate* each phase — so you can make your writing *systematic*.

Don't think of Tweaking as rewriting. You've already done that in the Strengthen section. You've made your ideas tangible, and you've reworked them until they flow smoothly — until the pace and the structure of your writing is working.

Instead, Tweaking is your deliberate manipulation of the specific choice of words, to guide the reader exactly where you want those eyes to go.

Tweaking comes last. Tweaking comes *after* your writing is working.

Even the most technical, scientific, left-brain analysis piece (the stuff you only read when you *have* to), is communicating an idea. Putting it on the page should be *automatic*. Instinctive. You can guide it, push it, steer it, move it, etc. But you need to let it flow.

Tweaking, however, is *not* automatic. It's conscious. Deliberate. Controlling.

You've always struggled with writing because you've tried to Tweak *while* you write. But not anymore. Writing FAST is simple. Tap into your brain (Focus), pour out your idea (Apply), shape it and mold it (Strengthen). And *then* start thinking about it, and making it work (Tweak)!

On your first attempts at the FAST System, don't be surprised if you start Tweaking during the Edit. Or when you Tweak, you might decide to jump back and do some more Editing or Strengthening. You need to get comfortable with each phase. And it'll take some practice.

But as you start *using* the FAST System on everything you write, you'll begin to make the separation.

You'll understand the philosophy of the Tweak.

It's all about the words.

Control the Ride

Imagine you were designing a rollercoaster. You wanted it to be the biggest, scariest, most lunch-revisiting ride thrill seekers ever dared to strap into.

You'd sketch it out. You'd create that enormous first hill that takes seventeen minutes to get up. Yeah. That would create panic in those faint hearts. You'd twist that first drop to get their little heads shaking around unnaturally. Uh-huh. That blast of terror would be palpable. You'd bend the tracks and spin them upside down and plunge them into a vertical drop, and then twirl them into curly-kews...

And then you'd look back over what you've done.

If *getting* them from the drop to the loop meant a long, straight, boring track, you'd tweak it. You might add a dip, for a quick stomach-drop. But if there was *too much* shaking and rattling and rolling — if there were no breathers to let lunch settle back down for a moment — you'd have to take out a few of the cliff-plunges, right?

With your writing, you're doing the same thing. And the first step is sharpening the "speed of the read." That doesn't always mean speeding it up! It might also mean slowing it down, so the reader can catch his breath.

To adjust that speed, we need to look at your writing a lot more closely. We need to look at each stretch of the track.

And create a Speed Plan — a plan to control the speed.

In the Strengthen section, you focused on the *idea*, and making sure it was getting across effectively.

Now, you're looking at your words. Your Speed Plan is focused on the language you're using.

Macro, Micro, Sentence

The Tweak phase has three steps.

Macro looks at the whole ride, and the *emotion* of your words. Look, your writing takes the reader on a ride, whether you control it or not. If lightning bolts aren't popping out of your words regularly, you won't hold those limited attention spans. In the Macro step, you *control the overall impact of the ride.* You feel the words themselves, and steer their impact.

Micro goes a step closer. It looks at the variety and placement of your words. Which pictures you're using, and how those words land on the page. The clearer and sharper your *images* are, the more interest the reader will have. Command attention with your writing. In the Micro step, you *control the details of the ride.* You deliberately guide the twists and turns.

And *Sentence* looks at the individual sentences, to keep the reader moving. Each sentence has to give the reader a reason to continue. And we do that with careful attention to each line. This is where we get very picky. In the Sentence step, you *fine-tune the dynamics of each sentence.*

In each of these steps, keep an eye on the words. We want to know their exact effect. Because the effect determines the strength of the lightning bolt.

By separating Tweak into these three steps, we can focus on each *aspect* of your words. In practice, you'll probably blend these three steps. That's fine. As long as you pay attention to each of them. Whenever you *struggle* during the Tweak phase, divide it up. Make it step by step.

Remember, the FAST System is a guide, not a rule.

It *simplifies* writing by making it a step-by-step process.

The rest of this chapter is about the Macro step.

The Words on the Whole

In the Strengthen section, you graded your work by looking at each chunk. And now that each chunk is working pretty well, it's time to go back over the whole thing. Only this time, you're looking at how the words *affect* you.

How they hang onto your eyeballs, and keep you reading.

Or do they?

Think of your writing as that rollercoaster ride. Except, rather than thrills and nausea, you're trying to give the reader your idea. And just like the rollercoaster, it's got to be a relatively smooth ride.

If you give your reader whiplash — either by throwing the wrong images out and confusing them, or by jerking their attention in different directions without warning — they'll complain. Or they won't keep reading (which is probably worse).

Now, part of it is pace. But pace isn't very specific. Pace is just the rate or speed your writing is being revealed at.

Instead, I like to think of it as the holistic effect of your words. In other words, do your words create the *feel* of the idea? Do they work with the whole? Or are they detached? Are you using some words and mental pictures here, and other kinds of images over there? Is it scattered?

If so, you reveal the idea at an awkward pace. It feels like something's wrong.

The whole and the parts aren't working together.

Read through your writing. Focus now on the overall effect of the words themselves. Not just the ideas — we've got them working. It's the words we're interested in now.

Now's your chance to be as harsh and critical as you want to be. Now's the chance to let the Movie Critic run riot.

As long as he keeps offering suggestions.

Impact Points

As you read your writing, look for what I call the Impact Points. These are moments that hit you. Moments of impact. When an idea is clear. Strong. And as a reader, it affects you.

Impact points stand out.

In fact, you'll be surprised. If you take a break between the Strengthen phase and the Tweak phase, something funny happens. You'll notice moments you *thought* made a strong impact which don't make any impact at all. And other spots leap out at you unexpectedly.

Make note of both.

As you read, you'll get a sense of the flow of your own writing. You'll feel like you're on that rollercoaster ride.

And just when you were expecting a turn — really *wanting* the turn! — it went the other way. And, frankly, it was disappointing. (There's nothing worse than a rollercoaster that lets you down. Same goes for writing.)

When that happens, make a note on your pages. I jot a big star next to the spot I *wanted* an impact point that wasn't there. And I use a small X for areas that *have* a nice impact point, and a small "–" for a *mediocre* impact point.

But don't stop! Keep reading. Let the words and images wash over you. You need to keep the flow of the ride. By quickly jotting down a star, or an X or a hyphen, you can come back and look at it after you're done.

And keep your BIN handy! Once you see trouble-spots, your mind quickly fills with ideas to fix it. Drop them in the BIN and keep going. You need to get a sense of the ride.

Afterwards, you'll look more closely at each of these areas, and rework them using the techniques in the next chapter.

Beyond Instinct

As you focus on the impact of the words themselves, a curious thing happens.

You'll start to develop an instinct.

It comes with time, and I'm not going to pretend it'll happen automatically the first time you start writing. But it develops much more quickly than you expect — *if* you approach your writing with an open-mind (non-judgmental).

You'll start to develop the ability to "feel the read."

Yeah, yeah, I'm sure it sounds like I've gone off to play with the fairies. But I'm serious.

Close your eyes and imagine running your finger over the roof of a car that has a rough finish. The paint job is peeling. You can feel that sensation in your fingertips, right? Now imagine the same car with a *smooth* finish. You glide your hand over it, feeling for every scratch or ripple. But it just slides.

You'll be doing exactly that when you read. Glide your mind over its finish, and feel for every scratch or ripple.

Instinct takes you a long way. As you put your words onto the page, you did it quickly, without judging it, without controlling it. You tapped into your gut instinct.

When you "feel" the read for scratches and ripples, you're looking for those spots where your instinctive communication skills didn't quite live up to the idea.

Sharpening the speed of the read is about deliberately smoothing those bumps into a sparkle.

The Speed of Emotion

As you glide your hand over your writing during the Macro step, you're looking specifically for the *emotion* of your words.

How does the ride *feel*?

Even writing whose sole purpose is to "convey information" still makes its mark through emotion. I'll prove it. Think of the last time you discovered something you didn't know. How did you *feel* about that? There's an "Aha!" moment. Or at least a momentary sense of *satisfaction* at the discovery.

If you've never noticed it before, pay attention to it. Think about your own ride through this book. Hopefully, you've had lots of moments of inspiration. Of excitement. Of anticipation.

That's what you're looking for in *your* writing, too.

Make notes. Is the emotion coming too slowly? If so, we'll need to tighten up that part. If your reader isn't experiencing *any* emotion in your work, they'll slow down, get bored, and turn off. Sharpen the *speed* of the emotion (the rate of its impact), and you'll keep your reader glued to your words.

Alternatively, is it firing along too quickly? The human mind can't handle rapid-fire emotional input. Too much emotion, and we shut off. If you're expecting your reader to stay excited or intrigued *the whole time*, they'll resist. You'll need to fill your writing out. Keep the ride smooth.

Now that you've Strengthened your writing, and everything's got a Tweak grade, you can finally *feel* the ride.

When you've gone through and marked up the impact points, you can create a Speed Plan, just like you created the Strengthen Plan. Line by line. Exactly how to fix it.

Give yourself a roadmap for the Tweak.

And don't jump the gun. Our whole goal is to see what we've got *first*, and fix it with a clear head.

For the first time, you can see your writing as a reader. And when you do, you can create a ride that'll dazzle them.

Sharpen Your Read Speed in 5 Easy Steps

Congratulations on getting to the Tweak phase. You let go. Be proud! And now you'll steer the words. Here are the five easy steps for tweaking the Macro level of your project.

1. <u>Re-read refreshed</u>.
   Take a break before you do this. Don't go directly from the Strengthen phase into this one. Your brain might fall out of your head. Get some distance, so your words can affect you. When you're refreshed, then:

2. <u>Take the ride</u>.
   Read through your work, and let it wash over you. Don't fix or adjust. You're not focused on the ideas anymore (those work already). Pay attention to the *ride* the words take you on. And as you do:

3. <u>Find the missing impact points</u>.
   Any time you expect a different *impact* to what you get, jot it down. If you expect a bang and get a whimper, make a note. Don't stop, though. Jot a quick symbol and keep reading. Hang onto the flow. When you're done, then:

4. <u>Fill and tighten</u>.
   Go back through your pages and expand the symbols. Make notes. Anything that has "too much too quick" needs to be *filled*. Anything that drags or crawls along needs to be *tightened*. When you've got your notes, then:

5. <u>Create a Speed Plan</u>.
   Like all your plans, this one is as detailed or as simple as you like. Determine where you need to steer, and give yourself the map to get there.

As you read, respond instinctively. Depending on your deadlines, do this twice, or three times. Use freshly printed pages each time, and take a break between each read. You'll respond differently each time you read it. Notice similarities.

In the Strengthen phase, we made each element effective. Now, you're judging the impact, and spotting where to hone.

And so...

Tweaking is the fine art of making your words glow. Making them so gripping and so magnetic your reader can't help but keep reading.

Only then can you shoot that lightning bolt out from the words on your page...

...like *THIS!!!*

[Imagine a bolt of lightning shooting out of this page and into your brain right now.]

Make sense?

(Wouldn't it be great if I actually *could* shoot a lightning bolt out of the page into your brain? Boy, *that* sure would help you grasp the goal. Oh, well. Guess I just have to wait for technology to catch up to me... *again*.)

Look. You got here.

You've barreled through some major milestones. So let's not drop the ball now.

Keep moving quickly.

Don't over-think, and don't let yourself get into such a hyper-critical state that you can't keep moving forward.

Remember the rule: Don't get stuck.

Feel the ride, and keep moving.

In the next chapter, we'll look at dozens of ways to grab those eyeballs and keep your reader hooked.

For now, get a sense of the flow.

We're about make it fly.

14

Techniques that Command Attention

If I was standing in front of you right now, I would extend my right arm. And between the tip of my index finger and the tip of my thumb, I would hold a ballpoint pen.

When you saw me extend my arm, you'd wonder what I was doing. It's not really natural for me to hold my arm out like that.

I'd ask you to look at the pen. For a moment, you'd think maybe the pen was going to do a trick. Turn into a rabbit, perhaps?

But you'd realize, no, that's not it. It must be something else.

Saying nothing, I'd continue to stand in front of you with my arm outstretched. The pen just sitting there. Quietly.

Gradually, you'd look me in the eye, growing tired of the game, and waiting for me to get on with it. Praying I'd do whatever I was about to do and just be *done*. You'd start to fidget.

I know this is true because I did it in my workshops.

I'd stand there, watching people's reactions. It's remarkable how quickly people grow impatient. Within minutes, the human mind is uncomfortable, and needs new stimulation.

And then, when you least expect it, I'd *drop* the pen.

Do you know what *you'd* do?

Guess. Take a guess before you read on.

I'll tell you exactly what you'd do.

You'd *watch the pen fall to the ground*. Even if your eyes had been locked on mine, your attention would instantly snap over to that pen, so you could watch it fall.

Know why?

Because the human eye is drawn to *motion*. It's why action films are so popular, even if they're vacuous. It's why kids love video games, and don't like reading books — nothing moves!

See, way back in Ooga and Booga's day, we had to watch for predators and hunt for food. Our eye evolved, until it could detect the slightest motion almost instantly. Notice it sometime. Notice how keen your sense of motion really is.

Oddly enough, this also translates to the page.

And not just with word pictures and action. We can also *create* that sense of motion through variety and the unexpected.

And that's what this chapter is about.

Commanding as much attention with your words as I did with a pen.

Spice and Variety

We all know the old cliché that says "variety is the spice of life." But when it comes to your writing, variety *is* life.

This book has over 60,000 words. Imagine if I'd used the same three types of sentences over and over and over again. Your brain would go numb. It would lose its mass — turn from solid to liquid, and start sloshing around in your head. Bo-ring!

Or worse! What if I only used one metaphor the whole way through? You'd go stir crazy. Imagine if every sentence — no, I mean *every single sentence* — used that "lightning bolt" metaphor. Oh man. You'd want to shoot me! And next time you were in an electrical storm, you'd curse my name!

(In fact, I recently read a book in a popular series that did exactly that. The author used a metaphor in his title, and then just beat it to death. By about page 30, you want to let a pack of wild dogs loose on the guy.)

The human brain needs repetition. Our most effective method of learning (aside from physical and emotive *experience*), is repetition.

But repetition is only effective in small doses (Get it? Get it?! *Get it?!*), or when you've added sufficient variety between those repeated instances.

An example would be something I've been repeating throughout this book: All writing is communication. It's an idea that's so central, I want to keep bringing your mind back to it. And each time I do, I add something *new*. That way, it *builds*.

As you look over the words you've written, start looking for variety. Hunt down and weed out any excessive repetition. When you start writing fast, repetition is unavoidable. And that's okay. But now, just *change* your words. Add color and spice and variety and flavor. Give the reader enough mental and emotional stimulation to keep her eyes moving.

To do that, let's tuck a few tricks up your sleeve.

Visual Imagery

Notice the last segment. I ended it with a visual image ("tuck a few tricks up your sleeve").

When a reader comes across a visual image, she can't help it. She'll picture the image in her mind, every time. Even if she tries not to. I'll prove it.

I'm about to give you a visual image. I want you *not* to picture it. *Avoid* letting the picture take shape in your mind. You'll see. No matter how strenuously you try to prevent it, the image will pop into your mind anyway.

Ready?

Try not to imagine this: a tiny little house with a bright red front door. And while you're at it, don't let your mind picture the enormous tree standing out front, dropping leaves across the lawn. Oh, and be sure to avoid seeing the image of a woman in her eighties, happily raking up the leaves, as the breeze gently tosses her white hair.

C'mon, be honest. You saw it all. And I didn't even go into any detail!

Fact is, it's impossible *not* to see it, unless you skip the paragraph entirely.

It the nature of words. The whole function of a word is to put a picture in your head. So *reading* words about pictures makes them pop into your head!

Use this.

When you're trying to express an idea, it's easy to get lost in the words. It's easy to ignore your words' visual impact. But your ideas dance around in your reader's imagination. When the pictures are sharp, your ideas are clear.

The key is to be specific. Avoid vagueness.

Specific nouns and action verbs work best. For example, I said "tree," above. But that's vague. Is it an "oak tree" or a "gum tree"? Does it have a thick trunk with bushy leaves, or empty dead branches that flick outward in all directions?

And I said the tree is "standing" out front. By swapping that for an action verb, I can make the picture much clearer. How about the tree is "looming" or "withering" out front? Each word gives a different image.

Be specific. See what you've written. And now that you're at the Tweak stage, make your pictures vivid.

Metaphors and Analogies

As our language evolved over tens of thousands of years, human beings developed a way of communicating that is unlike anything exhibited by any other species.

We use metaphors and analogies. And it has thrust human consciousness forward more dramatically than any other single facet of our nature.

A metaphor is the use of one idea or concept to represent another.

"Love is a battlefield." Or "women are roses." Or "that book is a dud." Each of them uses one thing to represent another. Love isn't *literally* a battlefield, but by making the comparison, we grasp the writer's idea. Women aren't *literally* roses, but the comparison evokes an image, which shapes your idea of what a woman is.

"The book is a dud" is even more subtle in its comparison. A dud is a bomb that fails to explode. It's something that is completely ineffective in its sole task. To make the comparison with a book is to draw that parallel — it's completely ineffective!

These analogies and metaphors are fundamental to human communication. If I wanted to explain the concept of "orbit" to you, I could hold up a golf ball, and say it's the moon. Then I could make a fist with my hand, call it the Earth, and then circle the golf ball around my fist. In your mind, you'd understand the concept of "orbit" because your mind can grasp the analogy and imagine the Moon orbiting the Earth.

This is fundamental to the way we communicate.

And you can use it directly.

Strong writing uses the tools of the language. Creating metaphors (like the lightning bolt, the Idea Factory, the Oscar-winner, the Movie Critic, the rollercoaster, and so on) strike at the very heart of human communication.

If they're vivid enough — and clear enough for your reader to see the connection — they'll strengthen your work instantly.

When you focused your idea back in Chapter 4, you created a metaphor. You turned your intangible *idea* into a physical demonstration. You did it instinctively. Without prodding. Because that's how human beings communicate.

At the Tweak stage, look to the *words* you've used, and the choices you've made. Are you creating metaphors that paint pictures for your reader?

Suspense and Anticipation

Hey, on this topic of suspense and anticipation, I think you're gonna really love Chapter 17. It's got a few segments that just make the whole book "click." But I've got to warn you. If you try to skip ahead, it won't work. It won't make sense. It needs *all* the chapters before it to make it work.

See, this book is a puzzle. Just like the FAST System itself. Each step builds upon the last. So when you get to the end, it all snaps into place. And it'll take your breath away. Especially when it has time to sink in.

See what I'm doing? I'm building suspense. (Admittedly not very well, but you get the idea.) I'm trying to give you a sense of anticipation. Why?

Because if you look forward to what's coming, you'll keep reading. It's as simple as that.

Just be sure your payoff lives up to its setup! (And don't worry, the FAST System does. Although, if you're astute, you can see that I just did it again. I *love* doing that.)

The whole time you're reading, you're anticipating what's coming. Every word, every sentence, every segment, every chapter, every section. Anticipation. You think it's going *this* way.

But if the writer turns it — makes it go *that* way, instead — you stay intrigued. As long as she doesn't ignore those expectations and leave you hanging, you'll continue reading.

Your own writing needs the same thing. Read each sentence in your work, and Tweak the anticipation factor. Keep the reader guessing. Build the suspense.

As you re-read your work, ask yourself what the reader is anticipating at this point. Satisfy that expectation, but in a *way* he wasn't expecting, and he'll stay glued to your page.

Placement and Emphasis

You can crank your visuals up a notch by deliberately focusing on the placement and emphasis of your words — how and *where* they appear on the page.

Let's say, for example, you were writing a story about two kids that wouldn't talk to the old man living in the crumbling old house at the end of the block.

Let's focus on the old man. By creating strong visual imagery, you can paint a very scary picture of him. You can use metaphors and mystery to build your image.

But if you place the words poorly, the real *impact* of that image will be lost. For example, if you first showed the old man as a nice old guy pruning roses in the garden, and *then* have the kids walk terrified up the front walkway, then when he answers the door, it won't have any impact! We knew he wasn't scary because of the way you revealed it.

But instead, what if you *hide* the old man, and we never see him? The kids hear strange noises coming from inside the house. They tremble cautiously up the walkway. The anticipation builds. As they go to press the doorbell, they notice there *isn't* one. It's only a hole filled with spider webs. They knock on the door, but it's ajar, and it creaks slowly open. It's pitch black inside. And just as the boys are about to slink in...

Which way you go with it is up to you. But if the old man is gentle and warm, you've created an *effect* with your placement of that information. By emphasizing the images that play against it, you control the ride. And the reader keeps reading!

All writing has an effect. The more deliberately you place your words, the more you control that effect.

As you Tweak, watch for the placement and emphasis of your words. Control the sentences to paint the images that most effectively express your idea.

Time and the Temporal Shift

One last thing I want you to watch for is *time*.

As a writer, you have the ability to stretch time or speed it up, depending on the effect you're going for. And you need to do it intentionally.

Time is a concept. Not just hours, days, weeks, months, or years. Those are just ways to *measure* it.

Time itself runs through everything we do. And it's there, in every word you put on that page. In fact, if you're not aware of it, your writing's probably too slow. It'll be stronger if you speed it up.

For example, think back over what you've read from this book so far. Did any of the chapters seem "slower" than others? Anything sluggish or maybe a little tedious?

Hopefully I've done my job well, and you said "No."

But hey, I'm a realist. Depending on where you're coming from (and how well I've Tweaked my words), you'll fly through some sections, and others will feel like they're plodding along.

You can *adjust* that, y'know. On several levels.

You can speed up time or slow it down at will. For example, you can show Bob at his high school graduation in one sentence, and then show his retirement in the very next. You've just sped through fifty years! Or, you can describe each flap of a humming-bird's wings in such detail that you almost stop time itself.

But that's just one level. You can also *jump* time by interrupting a story with a flashback. Here I am today, but it reminds me of when I was twelve. And then I'm back *there* again. Or I can go forward into the future — where I might be in thirty years. Time is adjustable for the writer.

Are you *using* time to make your writing stronger?

But when I say you can adjust the *speed* of your writing, I'm referring to a different kind of time — your forward movement.

Are you keeping your ideas moving forward? Or are you rehashing them over and over? Forward movement is vital. For the reader, time slows down when you're not moving anywhere. Imagine being stuck on a train or in traffic. You've *seen* this part. You're ready to move on. It gets tiresome very quickly.

Transitions are a good way to carry you from one sentence to the next. Notice how often I start a sentence with "and" or "but." It's done deliberately, to keep drawing you down the page. So we don't get stuck in time.

If it's done effectively, it speeds the read. If it's done poorly, it slows things down by being repetitive.

My writing style may not be appropriate for what you're writing, so I'm not suggesting that it's the way to go. I just want you to be aware of *time* in your writing.

How are you using it? How does it flow? Make sure it's working *for* you instead of *against* you.

Tweak the words to create the effect.

Show Don't Tell

When I got to this segment, I had to laugh.

In my race to achieve the deadline, I've done too much telling, and not enough showing. Think about this book, and which sections were *sloooow*. Look closely. I'll bet I'm "telling."

As writers, our job is to create images in the minds of our readers. And the old writing cliché "show, don't tell" is the best reminder I can think of.

What does "show, don't tell" mean?

Quite simply this: If you *tell* someone something, you'll bore their socks off. If you *show* them, they'll get it.

If I *tell* you to how to write FAST, I'm forcing you to assume a passive role. You aren't actively participating. You're just listening. All you can do is nod or shake your head.

But if I *show* you how to use it, you're active. You're engaging it. You're seeing pictures in your mind, and feeling yourself go through the process. You're interacting.

Remember at the start of the book, I said that if you *experience* the FAST System (rather than just passively reading it), you'll get it? "Show, don't tell" is built around the same basic fact. Make your reader *experience* your writing.

Use all the techniques we've mentioned in this chapter. And reshape your Speed Plan to command your reader's attention.

Ask yourself how you can *show* what you've written instead of just telling it. How can you create an *experience*?

As you look over your writing, ask yourself with every line: *Is this showing or telling?* You'll see exactly what to fix.

Command Attention in 5 Easy Steps

Your Speed Plan is built around the flow. Command attention at the Micro level. Use the techniques in this chapter. Look for what's possible. And take it in five easy steps.

1. **Zoom in.**
   The Tweak phase is all about the words. It's time to rigorously analyze what you've got. You've felt the overall ride. Now zoom in to the moment-to-moment *effect* of your words. Once you're in there, then:

2. **See the richness.**
   The metaphors, the visual imagery, the sentence construction, placement, emphasis, time, variety, sense of anticipation. Watch closely for *how* you're presenting your ideas. And as you're reading:

3. **Question everything.**
   Is this the *best* way to express that idea? Can you sharpen it and Tweak it to make it golden? The goal is not "perfection." Rather, you only want to *challenge* what you've got. Make sure it's the best you can do. Then:

4. **Earn their interest.**
   Think of your reader. Her time is valuable. *Earn* her interest by keeping your writing moving. Hold her attention by stimulating her mind. Make notes in your Speed Plan. How might you Tweak your words? And then:

5. **Adjust the Speed Plan.**
   As ideas spark in your mind, adjust the plan. Make your roadmap as detailed as you can. But don't get stuck or dwell on it. Picture your rewrite clearly in your mind.

Commanding the reader's attention is the fun part. Your words are on the page. Now you simply twist and move and shift them around to create exactly the impact you want.

Review this chapter *after* you've reviewed your writing, and your mind will bounce with ideas. Blend those ideas into your Plan, and in the next chapter, we'll Tweak.

And so...

When you're first starting out, the ideas in this chapter might make you want to go back to the Strengthen phase (or maybe even the Focus phase). And I'll tell you a secret, as long as you continue reading.

That's perfectly okay.

See, that's only going to happen the first two or three times you use the FAST System. And I want your writing to be as powerful as you can make it. So please do what you gotta do.

But the more you practice using the FAST System, the more these ideas (and others still to come) will be a part of you. You'll understand the essence of the job at hand.

And when you do, you'll find your own way to personally modify the FAST System for your own style and preference.

Using the FAST System the way it's designed, however, means applying all these ideas *last*. It means going through the System instinctively, and only steering the ship at the very end.

That way, you let your ideas out.

And then you perfect them.

And in doing so, you reach lightning speed.

15 Quicken and Polish

At last. You made it.

The final step in the FAST System. The last action of the Tweak phase. You're almost there!

In this chapter, you'll zoom in even further, to make sure *every word* is as crisp and dynamic as you can make it.

And then you'll *apply* your Speed Plan, and watch your writing go through the roof!

Sure, you've still got work to do. But you're coming into the home stretch now. It's exciting, isn't it?

Use that energy to push you through the last section.

I want you to notice something — notice *how* you got here.

The FAST System separated each job into its own designated task. And instead of trying to do everything at once, you were able to push through each phase at a time, and get words written.

That's a massive discovery.

See, when you *know* you've got the Tweak phase waiting for you, you *allow* yourself to let go. Your brain suddenly starts working together. In harmony. Left meets Right, they shake hands, and there is peace in the Factory.

And you can finally *complete* the projects you start.

So do it. Push that little bit further and *finish* it. I know you're anxious. We all get a little scared because "completion" means exposing ourselves to criticism.

But don't worry. We've got one more level of detail to look at before we're done. One more level to Tweak.

The Fine Print

The final step of the Tweak phase is making sure every word works, and is up to speed. New writers underestimate the importance of this stuff. Seasoned writers *over*estimate it.

The truth is somewhere in the middle.

Fact is, your writing is a reflection of you. And readers — especially of professionally-written material (like books, magazine articles, screenplays) — expect a certain level of quality.

If you don't meet it, they don't trust what you have to say.

Think about it. If some guy told you he was a professional athlete, and then you saw him huffing and puffing as he climbed a hill, would you believe him? Of course not!

Even if you're not writing professionally, your words are a measure of how well-spoken you are. If it's filled with technical mistakes — spelling errors, grammatical mistakes, and obvious "thought" errors — you don't think, *Wow, this guy's a bad writer.* No. You think, *Jeez, is this guy stupid?!*

It's not always fair. I've seen intelligent and well-spoken writers whose ideas are brilliant. Their writing is bold and dramatic. But their spelling is terrible, the punctuation is all over the place, and as a result, they can't get their work read.

Demand perfection. Don't send anything out before it's ready. Word choice and writing style can be forgiven, as part of your unique voice. But mistakes are the mark of an amateur.

(And on a sidenote: If you notice any typos or errors in this book, send me an email. If you're the first to point it out, you'll get a free gift.)

Before you send anything out, do a "Sentence-Level Tweak." Inspect every single sentence to make sure it's flawless.

Spelling and Grammar

This book is about the FAST System. It's about the *approach* to writing — not the rules of the English language.

So I'm not going to cover the details of good spelling and grammar. There are hundreds of excellent resources out there already (and plenty of *free* resources on the internet, too).

What I want to do instead is give you some insight into what you're looking for. What you *must* look for!

Correct spelling is crucial. A misspelled word either has a *different* meaning to what you thought, or it conveys a different *idea* to what you're intending.

So forget spellcheck on your computer. It's a start, but it's not foolproof. It misses a ton of words.

For example, if you say "accept" instead of "except," your spellcheck won't notice. But your meaning just changed entirely.

Always manually check your spelling. And if you're not good with that sort of thing, get someone else to do it for you.

Same goes for grammar — the *rules* of writing. Nouns and verbs need to be in the right places, or else you kill the flow.

If you know anything about grammar, you know I break some of the rules. Often. (Like that!)

Here's my rule of thumb: You can only break a rule if a) you *know* the rule, and b) you've got a good reason for breaking it.

I use sentence fragments. Intentionally. Because I want my writing to feel like I'm *talking* to you. In person.

But aside from those fragments (and sentences beginning with conjunctions), I obey most of the rules of grammar. Why? It's efficient! Good grammar tends to be smooth, fluid writing.

As you Tweak your work, scour it for spelling and grammar mistakes. And if you don't know the rules, learn them!

Paragraphs and Length

Short paragraphs are easier to read.

It's true.

Consider these paragraphs.

They're easier than those big blocky ones above, aren't they?

Of course.

But that doesn't mean you should write one-line paragraphs. In fact, it's generally rare, and used only for effect. Typically, a paragraph is one complete nugget of an idea. You start with an opening sentence, then hit the meat of the idea with one or more sentences, and then end it with a closing sentence.

But watch out for enormous paragraphs that stretch down half the page. Thick, dense, wordy paragraphs are hard work to read (unless it's a novel). Break them into smaller ones instead.

Paragraphs break up the page, and allow the reader to pause.

Now, different types of writing have different requirements, and I'm not saying all writing should look like mine.

I only want to call your attention to it. As you Tweak your work, pay close attention to the length of your paragraphs, and the impact it has on your idea. Are you forcing your reader to struggle through your writing? Or are you using it effectively?

It's not just about shorter paragraphs.

It's about paragraphs that keep the reader reading.

You need to do what's appropriate for the material.

And only *you* can know what that is.

Sentence Construction

And everything you've been noticing about your paragraphs applies at the *sentence* level, too.

In fact, the construction of the sentence itself can turn your words from boring ramblings, into powerful bolts of lightning!

It can single-handedly hold (or lose) the reader's interest.

It's beyond the scope of this book to look at all the finer points of sentence construction (like nouns, verbs, complements, modifiers, conjunctions, prepositional phrases, and so on).

But to give you a quick idea, consider this sentence:

"The Japanese man waits for a bus."

By playing around with it, you can change its impact.

"For a bus, the Japanese man waits." What effect does this have? Could it change the *feel* or the *meaning* of a paragraph?

Take a joke, for example. A punchline always serves up the "kicker" at the end.

Henny Youngman's classic line was "Take my wife — please!" The first three words sound like a setup, as in "Take my wife, for example... " But it twists at the end. "Please" turns the meaning upside down, and gets a laugh. (Well, it did in its day, anyway.) If you said, "Please take my wife," the joke would rely on performance instead. It's a subtle difference. And that's what you need to look for in your own work. Put your words in order!

Be exacting. Use the most effective words in the most effective way. It doesn't take much time to learn these things.

But it *will* take practice.

If you don't know these finer points of the English language, it's no excuse. Learn them, and keep moving forward!

Vague, Cliché, Unnecessary

As you're sifting through your sentences, it's the perfect time to weed out anything that's vague, cliché or unnecessary.

Vague sentences are bland and general, and have no direct meaning or point. They're filler. They don't say much, or they aren't specific. Every sentence should be there for a reason!

Clichés are sentences that have been done to death. They're not always bad — sometimes it's a quick, direct way to convey an idea. But the whole problem with a cliché is that we've heard it before! Use them too often, and you'll bore your reader.

Unnecessary sentences add nothing to your work. You've either said it already, or you don't *need* to.

When you write with lightning speed using Talktation, you'll write every kind of problem sentence. But you aren't thinking! So it's a *good* thing to do!

But now it's time to reach your hands in there and yank them out. They served their purpose. They helped you get your project written. But *reading* them will put your reader to sleep. So they've gotta go.

The best way to fix them is to either combine sentences, trim sentences in half, separate sentences, or just delete them entirely.

I also like to test every sentence against the "one idea rule." If you've got more than one idea in a sentence, it's too long.

That'll kill run-on sentences that go on forever and ever.

Make *every* sentence add something new to picture.

The Importance of Doing This Last

Here's a quick story as you start applying your Speed Plan.

As you know, when I wrote this book, I created a deadline for myself. And as my way of forcing myself to get off my lazy butt and get it written, I *advertised* the deadline.

But as my deadline raced towards me, I started feeling the pressure to do it right "the first time." I felt like I needed to craft beautiful sentences that rolled trippingly off the eyes.

And I got stuck. Big time.

I was so overwhelmed with trying to create perfection, that I couldn't write *anything*.

Eventually, my deadline was coming at me *so* fast, I *had* to let go. And I did. And whatever garbage first came to mind, that's what I'd put on the page.

Later, I discovered that a) not everything I wrote was garbage after all, and (more importantly) b) even if what I wrote *was* garbage (and there was a lot of it), just reading it back in "fixing mode" sparked ideas on how to change it.

And the later ideas were *always* sharper and clearer. Know why? Because the first time through, you're filling pages. But when you're Tweaking, you're improving what's already there.

So relax. Trust yourself. Embrace it. Jump in!

Even as you Tweak, remember: You can always fix it later.

Knowing When to Let Go

As you train yourself to write FAST, you'll break the habit of over-perfection. But when you're just starting, you'll have what I call Completion Anxiety.

Completion Anxiety is the fear of putting your work out there. You delay finishing because you're afraid to show it to anyone. What if they hate it, and then hate *you*?

So you keep fiddling, and never *complete* it.

You *over*-Tweak.

Instead, focus on *technicalities*. Spelling, sentences, paragraphs. Don't Re-Focus or Strengthen. You've done that stuff.

Just Tweak, and move on.

When you're done Tweaking the technical stuff, *get feedback*. Tell yourself you can always change it after the feedback.

But you *must* let go of it and get an opinion. The longer you work on something, the less objectivity you'll have.

Feedback can help you reclaim your objectivity.

Completion Anxiety is a simple fear of the unknown.

But I'll make it known for you: Not everyone will like your writing. Some will love it. Others will hate it. *Most won't care.*

People are focused on themselves. As long as you've made the idea clear, they're already on to the next thing.

So let go. Put your work out there when it's the very best you can make it — when you read it *knowing* you've steered those eyes, and polished those words.

Let it go when lightning bolts are leaping off the page.

Quicken and Polish in 5 Easy Steps

Finally, the Sentence-Level Tweak, and blasting through your Speed Plan. With the ideas and springboards in this chapter, and these five easy steps, you'll make your work read *fast*.

1. Touch each word.

As you read through your writing, literally, touch each word with your pen or finger. Check *every* word. You'll spot spelling mistakes, and review every thought. Then:

2. Watch like a hawk.

Hunt for grammatical errors. Look for new, more interesting ways to phrase a thought. Notice vague sentences, and paragraphs that stretch on forever. Make notes of ways to fix them. And then, finally:

3. Apply the Speed Plan.

Now that you've got detailed notes showing you exactly *where* to go, it's time to *go* there. Rewrite. And when you're finished, recycle through the Tweak phase again, fine-tuning even more. Until you've nailed it. And then:

4. Let go.

This isn't the end of road, it's a specific step. And if you don't do it, you could correct and fix and fiddle forever. If you've taken the FAST System step-by-step, your writing's pretty solid by now. It's time to:

5. Give it to your reader.

For smaller stuff, you're probably done. For longer stuff, send it out for objective feedback, and then consider the response. Adjust if needed. When it matches *your* idea, take a bow. You've just written with lightning speed.

Completing a major writing project is the most gratifying experience you can imagine. You started with nothing, and ended up with something that's really very good.

Always *complete* projects you start. If you don't, your self-doubt feeds on itself. As you cycle through the Tweak phase, focus on *technical* issues. Push to the finish line.

And so...

If you're anything like me, *starting* a project is infinitely easier than *completing* it.

So as you get to the Tweak phase, you start to get Completion Anxiety. You're afraid it's not good enough. You might start picking your words to pieces. Maybe you'll even make excuses for delaying the finish.

But here's the secret of the Tweak phase:

You can always do it again!

See? There's no pressure at all. So forget perfection. Keep your focus on your *reader*. Make the idea is clear to *him*. Push through it. And then get feedback on your work.

Completing your first major writing project is a revelation.

For me, writing this book has taught me things about myself I never knew.

And I've discovered things about my *topic* I never knew!

For example, not only does the FAST System *work*, every problem I ran into — *every single one!* — came when I ignored the system. When I leaped in without planning. Or tried to do three things at once (usually because of my looming deadline!).

As long as you keep coming back to it, the FAST System helps you actually *finish* your project.

And when you do, you reinforce a very powerful idea in your mind — the idea that "I can do this."

So keep powering through.

Finish this one and move on to the next.

Always put your reader first.

Tweak your words to give him the best possible ride.

And do it FAST.

Because I'm sure you have plenty more ideas to share.

[The Payoff]

66 Knowing is not enough;
we must apply.
Willing is not enough;
we must do. 99

—Goethe

16 The FAST System in the Real World

Focus. Apply. Strengthen. Tweak.

That's the system.

And now that you understand it, let's kick it into overdrive.

I want you to become a writing *machine!*

All in all, the FAST System is pretty simple. You take the complex process of writing, and break it down into phases. And then you break those phases down into steps.

And when you systematically move through each step, you'll finish *any* writing project quickly and easily. With more clarity. More impact. And a stronger *effect* on your reader.

But before you leap into it, wait for the Payoff.

In this section, I'll show you how to *maximize* the FAST System. This is where the final puzzle pieces snap into place.

In this chapter, we'll look at how FAST fits into the real world, and your everyday life.

Then in the next chapter, I'll show you FAST's most *powerful* technique. Plus, extra ways to get the most out of the system.

And in the final chapter, we'll push it all to lightning speed.

Look, I *know* what's waiting for you when you *finish* a major project. The sense of accomplishment. The satisfaction. The burst of energy that gets you focused on the *next* one!

The FAST System will get you there.

But FAST itself is just a system. It needs *you* to operate it.

And when you do, watch out.

A lightning storm is about to erupt.

The Battle Against Time

A couple short chapters from now, you'll finish this book. And as you leave its little cocoon, all the interruptions and chaos of life will come flooding back into your mind.

The "real world" returns.

And, suddenly, you'll be pressed for time, again.

We *all* are. Time is life's scarcest commodity. So we race into things, scrambling to finish at breakneck speed.

Heck, it's probably the reason you *got* this book!

But we run into a real danger.

The danger of charging in too fast.

See, life is an incredibly short adventure. Each of us has an astoundingly small window of time in which to achieve everything we will ever accomplish.

So what we *do* — even though we *shouldn't* — is leap headlong into things, fighting *against* time every step of the way. We think, *I've gotta get this done NOW, before it's too late!*

And we rush in, and get lost.

But the way to conquer time is to work *with* it, instead of *against* it. To *harness* it, and ride it like a horse.

The reason FAST works, is not because you're racing through it. It's not because of the speed writing techniques. That's only a very small part of it.

It works because it's *methodical.*

Because you know you want to write that thing. You know you want to finish by a certain date. And with the system, you can place each part of the job into its own block of time.

You plan it. You move through. Step by step.

You don't *beat* the clock — you *assign* it.

And that's how you win this battle. It's the only way to beat it. It's the only way to write *fast.*

But you've got to *do* it!

It's easy to read a book like this, think about it for a week or two, dabble with some speed writing, and then put it out of your mind. Life will *always* throw you distractions.

The only way to avoid that — the *only* way — is to begin applying the FAST System *immediately.*

Put it into practice. Into your daily routine.

Short-form Writing

The quickest and easiest way to get the hang of the FAST System is with short-form writing.

If you've already got plans for books, novels, screenplays, or other long-form writing, by all means, go for it.

But if you're hesitant, start small. It's like a test-drive.

So what's "short-form"? It's... well... anything *short*.

To me, "short-form" is anything less than twenty pages. But *you* might say "anything less than *five* pages," or even "anything I can finish in a week." Or *one day!* The definition is up to you.

Let's look at an example, to see how it works in short-form.

Say you want to write a one-page letter to Uncle Bob, about what's been happening lately.

Here's how you might use FAST to break it down:

Focus. You start by deciding what to tell him. Let's say you want to share the news of three recent events. What shape will they take? As you think about it, you decide a *theme* could tie the events together. Yeah. You'll share a *lesson* through the update.

Apply. Once you've mapped it out, you set checkpoints at one third and two-thirds of the way down the page. Then using Talktation, you blast through it. As fast as you can.

Strengthen. When you're done, you re-read it. Can you improve it? Maybe you decide to shift the first two events around, because it builds better that way. Get it flowing nicely.

Tweak. Finally, you sift through it. You chop sentences in half. Adjust the word order to make it more punchy. Tighten the imagery. Double-check your spelling.

And *bang!*, you're done.

How easy is *that*?!

It worked, because you knew the end result. You set yourself a timeframe. You decided on the idea, and you tore through it.

And *then* you looked back over it and tightened it up.

Using the FAST System on short projects is quick and easy.

If you only did this *once* a day, your speed would increase exponentially within a week. Letters, pamphlets, emails, ads, notes, *whatever*. Break them down. Do them quickly.

Your short-form writing projects are done in no time at all, and you're getting yourself ready for the big stuff.

The Long-form Writing Problem

This is what FAST was developed for. Long-form writing.

But long-form writing is a bigger challenge than short-form. And the main difference between the two is that long-form writing takes more *time* to complete.

Obvious, right? I thought so, too.

But it's not quite as clear-cut as it seems.

See, it's not just that there's more to *do*. It's that suddenly you have to factor in the *time* it takes to *do* it.

For example, take a book like this.

It's just not possible to write it in a day — I don't care *how* fast you write! It's gonna take days, weeks, or even months. So you've got to incorporate the project into your daily life.

But now you've got *two* things to manage: The *content* of your project (*what* you're writing) and the *timeframe* for its completion (*when* you're writing it).

With short-form writing, you can keep the whole thing in your head. But long-form writing is too big for that.

Take the letter you just wrote to Uncle Bob. It's short. You can start and finish in one sitting. As you're writing, you can see the end. You know *where* you are the whole time. You know you're ten minutes into it, and you've got ten minutes to go.

Mentally, each phase (F, A, S, or T) has a timeframe — it has it's own block of time. And it's got a *completion* time!

But with long-form writing, it's different. You know you're in the Focus phase, or the Strengthen phase, or whatever. But the *time* gets warped. How *long* will you be in the Strengthen phase? How *long* will it take to Tweak?

It's anybody's guess! And there's no set answer!

And it *will* be a problem for you. I guarantee it.

So be prepared. You need to know *where you are* in the process. And that means mapping out the *time*, too!

How? Determine how long the process takes you. Work on short-form projects to get a feel for it. Everyone's different. But *expect* the learning curve, so it won't surprise you.

For example, I've found that my *fastest* speed is actually slower than I thought. I write long-form projects *faster* when I allow more time for them. If I don't take enough time, I have to repeat the cycles (like the Strengthen phase) more often.

So by *not* planning properly, I go *slower* going faster! (How's *that* for a brain teaser?)

But I don't want you to get lost. So here's the way around it:

Set time aside for your writing. *Every single day.* Even if it's only twenty minutes. Get to know your optimal writing speed. Determine how long each phase takes you.

Then, once you know, you can *assign* the clock. You can give two weeks to the Focus phase, or eight weeks to the Strengthen phase, or whatever's best. That way, you'll know *where* you are in the process *as* you're writing it. And when you're six weeks into an eight-week Strengthen phase, you'll know if you're on target or not.

And if you're *not*, you'll be able to adjust.

Without getting lost.

Otherwise, life has a way of getting in the way.

Life's Little Distractions

Sitting (and keeping) your butt in a chair takes a certain amount of determination. I think we should get our heads together and develop some sort of glue. We could make millions.

Why is it so hard?

Because just as the human *eye* is drawn to motion, the human *mind* is drawn to stimulation.

That Idea Factory is cranking. Every idea in your head is sparking a hundred other ideas. The Factory's churning. It's looking for something new to process. To filter. To play with.

When it sees the same thing over and over, it gets bored. It wants something *else* to play with.

The longer the project, the more easily it gets bored.

And it *embraces* distractions. And that's a killer.

For example, even on days I *knew* what to write, even when I was *excited* about writing, and even when I *had* to get it written quickly, I would *still* let ridiculous distractions get in the way.

Today, I wanted to finish this chapter *and* the next two. But I thought of an example, and did a little research for it on the internet. I saw something funny, and got sidetracked.

I spent *three hours* looking up "time-wasters" on the web.

I couldn't believe it! And now it's nearing midnight, and I'll only have time to finish this *one* chapter.

Ridiculous.

As writers, we need to focus. We need to add to the page count every day. But distractions are a part of life. It's the way your brain works. The secret to handling them is this: Don't pretend they won't happen. Just prepare for them.

Allow yourself "distraction time"!

If you don't give your mind a bit of leeway, it won't stay focused. So write in short blasts, and surround those blasts with distractions. Or if you know it takes an hour to pound through five pages, give yourself *two* hours to do it. Pound through, get distracted, pound some more, get distracted... back and forth.

Just as you gave the Movie Critic his time, give distractions their time, too.

Otherwise, they'll get the better of you *every* time.

Motivation and Procrastination

But don't confuse *distractions* with procrastination. They're not the same. You might *entertain* a distraction *because* you're procrastinating. But they're two different things.

Procrastination is *avoiding* something you need to do.

And it's caused by one thing, and one thing only:

Fear.

On some level, you're afraid of what you're writing. Or you're afraid of finishing. Or of the *work* involved in finishing. It's not *terror*, so it doesn't *feel* like fear. But it is.

You're letting procrastination overpower motivation.

I'll show you how it works.

I've written this book in first person. Like a conversation. It's me talking directly to you.

I wrote it this way so that I could share my thoughts, my opinions, my ideas and my motivations with you. Personally.

Why? Because I need you to *understand* my motivations.

And it's not to satisfy my ego, or to talk about myself.

I'm sharing them so that — hopefully — you can see how vitally important *motivations* are to *your* writing.

Look, I never thought I'd write a book. I was only going to make movies. But when the big picture formed in my head — when I *saw* what was possible — the vision was suddenly clear.

I wrote this book to get *you* to write. And to get you *talking* about writing. To get you to tell *other* people about the book, and to get *them* writing, too. So that, eventually, this book would find enough readers who want to try screenwriting, that we can generate a ton of great scripts to turn into movies.

Understand this:

The only reason I've been able to *finish* this book — on a topic I never imagined writing about! — is because I have such a clear *vision*, that it's fueled me for two solid months.

I see this book completed. I see FASTscreenplay completed. I see the Screenplay Factory completed. And I see myself making movies with the 5% of people that apply this stuff.

And that's my *motivation*. It keeps me going, even when I've wanted to give up.

And *you* need it, too, for *everything* you write.

Because only motivation can kill procrastination!

You'll only complete a project when you have a clear vision of the *end result*. And you *keep* that vision in your mind.

The vision must be *stronger* than the fear.

And regardless of what you think of *my* vision — even if it's flawed or simplistic or unrealistic (or even if it doesn't pan out) — *without it*, I would never have written a word.

Understand this. Use it. Incorporate it.

It's the only way to fly.

Customizing FAST

Now, even though I think the FAST System is fantastic, I'm a realist. And I know that in the real world, you'll run into things you don't like about it.

Maybe a Speed Plan in the Tweak phase just doesn't work for you. You might prefer to go through and tweak *as* you're reviewing everything.

Or maybe the Focus phase actually gets in the *way* of your writing, or takes away some of the magic. Instead, maybe you prefer to just start writing. You like to see where spontaneity takes you first.

The FAST System is not a set of rules.

If anything, it's designed to help you through whichever part of the process is slowing you down.

Don't *assume* the Focus phase won't work for you. Or that the Speed Plan is a wasted step. Try it out as written first, and see how you like it. Put it to the test.

But at the end of the day, the FAST System is a guide. And I *want* you to customize it to your own taste. What works best for *you* will *always* help you write faster and better.

Never fight this system. It's helpful and intuitive. But if any part of it doesn't work, skip it and move to the next step. Make it the AFST System, if you prefer. Or the ASFT System? I still think FAST works best, but writing is a deeply personal thing.

However those sparks come out easiest, let them out!

You'll get better and better the more you write. I've seen it happen. I've watched people go through metamorphoses —from novices that take months to string a few average words together, to solid screenwriters that move through their work quickly.

Whatever helps you get there — use it. Build onto FAST. Incorporate your own techniques. If you've got one you'd like to share, let me know. Maybe I'll share it with everyone else who's reading this book.

The point is, FAST is a solid system. But it's flexible. Rigid rules get in the way of good writing.

Break free, instead.

FAST Means Fast

If there *is* one rule I don't want you to break, however, it's that FAST means *fast*. I didn't just pull an arbitrary acronym out of thin air. I know everyone's a little acronym-crazy these days. But FAST fits. It works beautifully.

Because the faster you write, the faster you'll write.

The speed of your writing feeds on itself. And that goes both ways — fast *or* slow!

Have you ever sat down to write, looked at a blank page, and couldn't come up with *anything*? You feel blocked. Your confidence goes straight down the tubes. And prying each word out is like wringing water from a potato with your bare hands.

It takes you half an hour to get three sentences you like. And because you re-read them constantly, it will take another half hour to get the next three, too.

Forget all that. Write fast. You can always change it later.

You can always fix it later. You can *always* improve it later!

I don't mean to sound like a broken record. But it's not enough to just "get" this. You've got to feel it in your *bones*. It took me so long to grasp this, I want to *force* it to stick in your mind: You can always, always, *always* change it later!

Pour crap onto the page. Write *fast!*

To plug into what you're really trying to say — to harness the power of that Idea Factory — you've got to open the doors. It's always easier to fix it, than to put it on the page in the first place.

So, please. Go fast. Through every step of this process. Through the Focus phase, the Apply phase, the Strengthen phase, and even the Tweak phase. Go as fast as you can.

If you truly apply each phase — if you really put the effort into *doing* it — the speed will push you through.

The FAST System on 20 Minutes a Day

In many ways, I think it's *better* to have less time to spend on your project. It forces you to move quickly.

Professional writers have an unfair advantage over the rest of us. They get to write full-time. And because they can devote more time to their writing than someone sneaking a few hours here and there, they get *better* at their craft more quickly.

You'll get better at *anything* you repeatedly do.

But they also have enough time to get stuck. And they have just as many interruptions as you do.

Would you love to write full-time? Imagine all that free time. Imagine having a six-month deadline, and knowing it'll only take three months, working three hours a day!

Sounds great, doesn't it?

Yeah. And it's fantasyland. Even if you *have* all day to write, urgent issues still come up. And always at the wrong time.

Life happens. You're desperate to make a chapter work, and the phone rings — you need to take the call. You need to deal with a customer. You need to run to the hospital. You need to go to that party you don't want to go to. And on and on.

Whether you have a full-time job, or no job at all, it's up to you to put *time* into your writing, and to make sure it gets done.

The FAST System works on as little as 20 minutes a day.

In fact, I recommend it!

Working in twenty-minute blocks does three things.

Firstly, it focuses you on the task at hand. If you know you've "only got twenty minutes," you're less likely to let distractions get in the way. You'll power through your writing.

Secondly, it removes excuses. You can't tell me you can't find twenty spare minutes in your day. You can. So you can write.

And thirdly, it keeps you fresh. Blast through for twenty minutes, and then walk around, clear your head, or get distracted. You don't go numb in the brain from staring at a computer screen for too long.

So whether you're a professional writer with all the time in the world, or a novice with two jobs, break it down into twenty-minute chunks, and let FAST help you power forward.

And so...

In the real world, you'll encounter all sorts of roadblocks to your progress. People will be jealous, some will even claim you just can't write as fast as I'm suggesting (at least not if you want to write well).

Every time you sit down to write, or to focus, distractions will leap in front of you.

You'll even discover things about the *process* of writing that you just don't like very much.

FAST will help you through all of that.

The whole point of the system is to break your writing down into small chunks, and then blast through those chunks as fast as you can.

Anticipate problems. Plan for complications. Make room for delays and the unexpected.

It, too, is all part of the process of writing.

And when you control it and send it where *you* want it to go, you'll accomplish every goal you set.

Most people never even *set* a goal.

But you've got a whole system for reaching them.

And it's about to get a whole lot easier.

17 Squeeze the Most Out of FAST

As I've been writing this book, I've been jotting down ideas. Ways to maximize the FAST System — to get the *most* out of it.

And I'm excited. I'm really jazzed about this.

Because Chapter 17 is where they come out — how to turbocharge your writing. It's got one *technique*, and six or seven *ideas* to kick it into overdrive, and get you running at full steam.

For me, it's a rush. It's *exciting* to think I might actually help you get your work written. That maybe (just maybe) ideas from *my* head might spark ideas in *yours*.

Call me simple. But I think that's cool.

If you're on your *second* read of this book (and you've been applying it), you must be *buzzing* right now! You've nearly finished your project. It's exciting, isn't it? See! I told ya!

But if you're on your *first* read of the book (still "getting your head around it"), you can see it now. You can see *how* this book will walk you through it. And you're ready to *try* it.

So I've got to warn you.

Part of your success with FAST is determined by *how* you implement it. Notice how I try to *encourage* you and *kick* you into gear! To help you get excited about this stuff!

Why? Because when you get *excited*, you accomplish more. When you raise your energy level, everything is easier. It's not just "positive thinking." If you put yourself in that frame of mind, your body gets physically poised to dig into your project.

So let's make it easy, and look at some reasons to *get* excited.

The Mental Pre-Flight

The FAST System itself is a step-by-step guide through each phase of the writing process.

But it's got an amazing side benefit, too.

By simply *understanding* FAST, you can break down *any* writing project in just two minutes.

Two minutes!

It's a technique I call the "Mental FAST System Pre-Flight." Or, simply, "the Pre-Flight."

It's the most powerful technique in this book, and I couldn't share it until now — until you understood how the FAST System works. And if you really *use* it, you'll break down new projects effortlessly, and prep yourself for the writing process.

And best of all, it feeds on itself. The more you do it, the more you understand it, the better you'll get.

The Pre-Flight is a visualization technique. But before you dismiss it as too "new age" for you, *try it*.

Here's how it works.

You're going to take two minutes, and *fly through your entire writing project in your mind*.

In other words, you'll visualize *each phase* (Focus, Apply, Strengthen, Tweak) unfolding in your imagination. Each phase gets thirty seconds.

Like this:

Thirty seconds watching yourself *Focus* your idea.

Thirty seconds watching yourself *Apply* that plan.

Thirty seconds watching yourself *Strengthen* your work.

Thirty seconds watching yourself *Tweak* the words.

You're not just "thinking about the Focus phase." You're really going *through* it — really *doing* the Focus phase — in full detail. See the whole phase unfold before your eyes.

Pretend you're watching a videotape from the future — and it shows what you've already *done*. But the videotape is running in fast motion. Like time-lapse photography.

You're not seeing selected *moments* from the Focus phase. You're watching the *entire phase* zip by!

For example, the first ten seconds, see yourself brainstorming. Capturing your idea in one sentence. Watch that whole process.

The next ten seconds, watch yourself making the idea tangible. See it zip by, as you create your Preview in your imagination. Then, the last ten seconds, watch as you stretch that idea across the Power Grid, and chunk out a Focus Plan with checkpoints.

Watch it *happen*. Watch yourself *doing* it.

"Pre-fly" through the entire project!

If you haven't experienced the FAST System yet, it might be difficult to imagine. And it's true — your *first* Pre-Flight is just your imagination.

But as you *experience* the FAST System — as you go through and use it on every project you write — your ability to visualize each phase gets stronger. The Pre-Flights get more "realistic." You start to *see* each phase, because you've been *through* it.

And an amazing thing happens.

You begin to go beyond mere imagination. Gradually, you start to *foresee* the project itself. The answers to your problems. The solutions to your ideas. You see the whole project — days, weeks, months — you *harness* it — in just *two minutes*.

You get your mind moving *fast!*

Don't underestimate this technique.

It's *not* airy-fairy. It's amazing. And if you really *do* this, your jaw will hit the floor.

Ideas will spark ideas in a ferocious lightning storm in your brain. And you'll develop the ability to crystallize those ideas and harness them quickly and efficiently.

It's a short-cut to nailing your project.

And it works.

Just as you'll Focus and plan your idea before you blast through it, the Pre-Flight lets you "Focus" the project itself.

And it only takes two measly minutes.

I guarantee you this. No matter how "new age" you think the Pre-Flight is, trust me on this one.

It's *this* technique that will change the way you write forever. How's *that* for a Payoff?

Quickly Break Down Anything

Can you see the pattern that's emerging?

The whole point of the Pre-Flight technique (and, indeed, of the FAST System itself) is to break big projects down *quickly*.

Listen, writing can have incredibly satisfying moments.

But it can also be pure, unadulterated *torture*.

For me, I've gone through *both* during the writing of this book. And I've noticed an interesting phenomenon.

The longer anything takes, the *harder* it becomes. And the harder it is, the more *torturous* it feels.

But what's even *worse* is that when it's difficult and painful to *write*, it also tends to be confusing to *read!*

Think back over this book. Were any chapters or segments confusing? Oddly enough, they're *almost certainly* the areas I struggled to write!

Same goes for your ideas.

Break them down *quickly*, and you won't have a chance to over-complicate them. Remember: Simple is *always* better.

Here's how to break an idea down quickly.

Do it by stripping the idea into its component parts.

For example, let's say your idea is "Absolute power corrupts absolutely." And you want to turn it into a novel.

What are its component parts? "Absolute power" is one part, "Corrupts" is another, and "Absolutely" could be the third.

Once you've identified them, immediately turn those components into examples.

For "Absolute power," you might create a character who's *got* absolute power. Or maybe one who *wants* it, instead.

For "Corrupts," you might outline a *path* of corruption — or two or three — leading from "honest" to "corrupt" (or from *corrupt* to *honest*).

For "Absolutely," maybe you'll find a visual example of something that cannot be undone — a human tragedy that brings this idea out.

Quick. Immediate. Decisions. Follow your instincts.

Use this example to spark your *own* ideas. To give *shape* to your writing. And the more you practice, the sharper you'll become.

I've found that it's *much* more effective to move quickly and instinctively through it, than over-think it. The ideas can certainly evolve *as you go through the process*. But when you over-think it early on, you prevent yourself from moving forward.

Break it down. Run the Pre-Flight. And then leap in.

When you do, the ideas in your mind begin to flow.

The Idea is the Key

And that's the key. *That's* how to squeeze the most out of this system. By keeping the point in front of you the whole time.

Throughout this book, I've been repeating a phrase.

I've even called attention to the fact that I'm repeating it.

You know what it is, right? Say it with me:

All writing is communication. All writing attempts to get an idea from *your* head into your *reader's* head.

Why do I keep saying it?

Because the idea is the key.

It holds everything you ever need to know about your work. If your writing is flat, dull, boring or repetitive, the idea isn't *full* enough. If your work is too far "out there," the reader isn't *grasping* your idea. If you're struggling with a section in the middle, you haven't completely nailed *how* it fits into the building of your idea — or how to *express* it.

The *idea* is the key to everything.

It's the question *and* the answer.

The Focus phase makes it tangible. The Apply phase gets it out. The Strengthen phase makes it stronger. The Tweak phase makes it work.

Sometimes it hits you instantly. Sometimes you can only *find* it through the very process of writing it!

But the point to grasp is this:

You don't need your idea at the start. But you *do* need your idea at the end. Without your idea, your communication is empty and pointless.

To squeeze the most out of the FAST System, it's vital to hammer away at your idea. To nail it down, and give yourself a way to hold it up for your reader to see.

That's the essence of writing. Communication.

Flexible Deadlines

My own experience with this book tells me two things.

First of all (to bend a famous quote), "Deadlines are a good thing, maybe the best of things, and no good thing ever dies..."

Without my self-imposed deadlines, you wouldn't be reading

these words. If you think you're a pretty snappy procrastinator, I assure you, I'm better. I procrastinated for five hours today! Even *after* I told you *yesterday* that I shouldn't do that!

Deadlines are incredibly valuable. So valuable, that I don't think you should even *start* a project without one.

But the second thing my experience tells me, is that by giving yourself too *narrow* a deadline, you cause undue stress. Unless you've got a hard deadline from an editor or professor or someone else leaning over your shoulder, make your deadline *flexible*.

I gave myself a five-week deadline for this book.

I planned three weeks to write (to Focus and Apply), and two weeks to rewrite (to Strengthen and Tweak).

Jeez. I was clueless. It wasn't anywhere *near* enough time.

Instead, it took four weeks to Focus and Apply it.

And as I approached the five-week deadline, my nights were sleepless, and my days were filled and worry. And it got worse.

When I started Strengthening (something I had never tried to do on a *book* before!), I discovered that it took me *considerably* more time than I expected.

I pushed back my deadline. And I didn't even set a new date.

I spent three weeks Strengthening and Tweaking.

And now that I'm done, I wouldn't mind another three weeks, to be honest.

The lesson is simple. Set a deadline. A *hard* deadline — and really push to get it done. (You'll never finish, if you don't.)

But don't go crazy in the process.

Particularly when you're just starting out (or writing a *style* you're not used to), keep it flexible.

The goal is to *train yourself* to write faster and faster.

Not to race to an early grave.

Some Phases Will Take Longer

We're all different.

Depending on your ideas, your temperament, and your own personal style, some parts of FAST will affect you differently than they affect somebody else reading this book.

And where I've given you examples, I run the risk of making it seem like *that's* the "right" way to do it.

My way is not the "right" way. *Yours* is.

Don't be surprised if the FAST System works differently to how you imagine it.

Maybe you'll spend more time than you thought you would on the Focus section. Or on the Strengthen phase. Or while you're Tweaking.

If your typing skills aren't up to speed, the Apply phase might take longer than you like.

It's okay. We're all individuals, and each of us needs to find his own way of writing. His own way of getting the words out.

One of the problems with writing this kind of book, is that I need to make it clear — without giving you a "standard."

There's no *right* or *wrong*. There's only *effective*.

If I say it would take four months to write a novel, don't hold that up as your standard. You have to try out the FAST System and see for yourself. How long will it take you? It could take twice as long. Or three times as long. Or more.

On the other hand, you might double that speed!

It's easy to get frustrated if you're not moving as quickly as you think you "should." (Or to think something's wrong if you're going twice as fast.)

Especially when you're first starting out, always assume it will take longer than you expect.

My estimate? Whatever you're estimating (the whole project, or just the Focus section, or just the Strengthen phase, etc.), determine how long you expect it to take. Not a bloated figure.

Estimate how long you *really* expect it to take.

If you finish in that time, fantastic.

But allow for at least *twice* as long.

And when you're first starting out, allow for *four times* as long. If all goes well, you'll finish when you first expected.

But if not, you won't lose your self-confidence because of it.

Fall in Love with Words

This is the very best way to squeeze the most out of FAST.

Most of the words we use today have a very long history. They've twisted and changed and distorted and contorted from one form into another over — sometimes — thousands of years.

Words evolve, and change meaning. Words get stolen from one language and adapted to another. Words get abbreviated, mangled, colloquialized, blended, coined, and invented. And sometimes re-invented.

And their meaning in any given sentence can be changed or determined by the other words that surround them.

Words are great.

And I mean *great*.

They're so great, we can come up with better words than "great"!

Fantastic, excellent, cool, tremendous, marvelous, terrific, dynamite, exceptional, dandy, awesome, sublime, glorious, outstanding, remarkable, splendid, peachy, exemplary, wonderful... and probably a hundred more.

Get excited by the possibilities of words and their many different nuances. With your writing, you can pinpoint an idea so clearly, so accurately, that it will physically transfer from the inside of your brain into the mind of another person, exactly as you intended.

Words are your tools. They can help you or hinder you.

Make them your friends.

No. Go beyond that. Fall in love! Notice words, and how they form sentences in *other* people's writing. Look for ways to improve your words, and make your ideas clearer.

It's a love affair that has *great* rewards.

No Comparison

At the moment, there are about 6.5 billion people running around on this planet. And every single one of them is unique. Because every single one of them is taking a different journey through the walk of life.

Your own journey has never been experienced by anyone else who has *ever* walked the face of the Earth. And no one that follows will take the same path, either.

So why do we compare ourselves to other people?

Our use of the language is unique, as well.

Sure, a writing style can be copied, or duplicated, or mimicked. But if we write in our own natural style, each of us will communicate in a way that's one-of-a-kind.

For example, I was raised in Los Angeles, but have lived in Australia and New Zealand for the past eight years. My style of speaking and writing is predominantly American, but with some very heavy Australian and Kiwi influences.

If you were raised in Melbourne, but moved to Sydney for six years, and then up to the Gold Coast, you would adapt to the local lingo. And it would blend into your own style.

But you're also influenced by people you've known and spent time with. You take on borrowed mannerisms — how *they* speak (and your *reaction* to how they speak), and what you've read, heard on the radio, and watched on television.

All in all, your voice is just about as unique as it gets.

If you don't know certain words (or never use them), they'll never enter your writing. If you've amassed a gigantic vocabulary, you'll draw upon it for unique shades of meaning.

One is not better than the other.

Whatever you write, however you have evolved, you are unique — not because it's a "feel-good" thing to say, but because it's true from a sociological angle.

Embrace it!

Naturally, your writing is for your *reader*, so you want to write it in a way *they* will understand. But if you don't use that unique voice, you're forever struggling against yourself.

Forget about comparing your writing to that of another writer. Appreciate writing you respect and admire. Enjoy it.

And master your craft as best you can.

But you are you. And your voice should reflect it.

Learn to Type

And one last tip for squeezing the most out of the FAST System is to learn to type.

One day, I'm sure voice recognition technology and tools will replace the need to manually enter words into the machine. But I've tried everything that's on the market today, and it's all generally terrible.

Plus, as a writer, I really think there's something to be said for manually typing each word. It's tactile. It gets you in *touch* with your words.

And I believe the Talktation technique has exactly the right level of "connection" between you and your words. Typing each word into your screen manually allows you to see, and ponder, and consider every word you write.

Speaking is easier, sure. But it's also easier to use throwaway words. Verbal communication has its own style and effectivenss.

Learning to type is easy.

You can learn the keyboard in a few short lessons. And in a few more — and with a bit of practice — you can be typing quickly in no time.

The faster you can type, the more easily you can transfer the thoughts from your head to the page.

Imagine if the instant a word became a thought in your head, you could have it on the page! You'll never get *quite* that fast (don't underestimate the speed of your mind), but you *can* get those fingers moving lightning quick.

Practice Talktation, and learn to type, and you've got one blazing-fast combo.

And so...

The FAST System is an *approach* to your writing. Its real power comes from your own *application* of it. Use your *mind* to apply it first.

By simply *thinking* about your writing in a different way (FAST) to how you've always thought of it (random and disorganized), you'll write faster than you ever have.

The same goes with this chapter.

By *thinking* differently about the system itself, and how you're going to approach it, you can expand its capabilities.

Truth is, you'll get as much out of this system as you put in. If you don't use it, you won't see results. But the *more* you use, the better those results will be.

The more you'll write. The more confident you'll become. The better you'll understand the FAST System itself. And the more you'll write. (And the cycle continues forever.)

It's all in your mind.

And lest we forget, the *mind* is your Idea Factory.

And it's a storm of ideas.

Use the Mental Pre-Flight. Fall in love with words. Find your own voice and express it.

I can feel the lightning buzzing already.

18 How to Reach Lightning Speed

The subtitle of this book is "How to Write Anything with Lightning Speed." And I've tried to gradually build on the lightning bolt analogy throughout this thing.

And you get it. You see it. When I refer to those bolts of lightning, you know I'm referring to your own *ideas*. And every time I repeat it, you know why I do. Okay. Cool.

But let's talk about the "lightning *speed*" analogy.

Chances are, you originally picked up this book because you wanted to write faster. Or because, like me, you struggle with the process of writing. And it takes forever.

So before we finish, I want to look at some specific ways to get you to actually *reach* lightning speed. Not just maximizing the FAST System, but *physically* writing faster.

I've seen a lot of writing students over the past four years. And statistically, only 5% of them ever *applied* the information. With a better *system* — like FAST — we should get better results.

But I'm not talking 10%. Maybe if this book sold a million copies, I could live with 10%. But c'mon. When was the last time you heard of a chart-topping book on *writing?!*

No. 10% isn't good enough.

I want 90% of readers to apply this stuff.

And statistically, that means *you*.

The faster you write, the more likely you'll actually *do it*. And when you taste success, you'll be inspired to continue.

So let's *reach* lightning speed. Here's exactly how.

Practice Makes Perfect

Sorry. But I had to.

It's a cliché. It's too basic. It's not what you wanted to hear.

Too bad. It's a cliché because it's *true*. Practice makes perfect. And the more you practice, the better you'll get.

In fact, you can *only* improve with practice.

When I was a kid, I used to play the piano. By all accounts, I was extremely talented. I had a natural flair for it, and I guess it came instinctively to me.

Today, I couldn't play the piano to save my life.

What happened?

My parents made me practice every day.

In the early years, when piano was fun, I *enjoyed* that daily practice. But as time went by (and my notoriously short attention span developed), I didn't want to practice anymore. But my folks were paying for the lessons (and, let's face it, I was good at it), so they forced me to continue.

But it turned sour. I grew to hate the piano.

It felt like punishment. So I quit after five years.

As an adult, I can understand why my parents made me do it. It's the only way to cultivate your skills. And, in retrospect, part of me wishes they hadn't let me stop.

Who knows how good I might've become?

The lesson here, is this: You'll only improve if you practice. But you'll only *practice* when you *enjoy* it, or when you see a *reason* to improve — like a goal you *want* to achieve.

Now that you have the FAST System — practice is easy.

Just dream up new ideas, and put them into motion.

With this approach, you write *fast*. You get the ideas on the page quickly, and improve them quickly, too. As you practice *with* the FAST System, the system itself helps you go ever faster. You improve without the struggle.

If you choose topics you *enjoy*, it doesn't have to be painful!

So enjoy it. And just do it.

Commit to yourself — you won't let this book be a waste of time. Commit to yourself — you *will* put your ideas into motion. You *will* turn them into writing.

Start small, have a blast, and practice. It's the only way.

Always FAST

You may have recognized it by now. But I want to call your attention to it anyway.

The "FAST" acronym is a mnemonic device. A memory tool. It's designed so that the *word* actually *triggers* the system.

Think about it. You want to write something. You want to finish it quickly. What are you gonna do?

Now that you *understand* the FAST System, it's almost impossible to look a writing project any other way!

Focus, Apply, Strengthen, Tweak.

Why *wouldn't* you use it?

So let's even go one step further.

Why not use the *word* to help you write?

Every time you see or hear the word "*fast*" — whether it's in print, in an advertisement, on the news, in conversation, or *wherever* — let it remind you to write. Let it inspire you!

Let the word "*fast*" — in *any* context — make you think of Focus, Apply, Strengthen, Tweak. Let the *word* spark a lightning storm in your mind.

If you really want to reach *lightning speed*, the trick is to make FAST feed on itself. The System — which gets better with practice. The Pre-Flight — which fuels the system.

And the word itself — which brings it all back to your mind.

It's been *designed* to feed on itself. Let it. Use it.

Notice how I've taken a common, ordinary, everyday word — a word that describes what you *want* — and turned the word itself into the most powerful writing tool you've got.

I want you to *write!* And to *keep* writing!

And to apply the word — the system — everywhere!

Apply FAST when you write your emails. Apply it when you write letters. Apply it when you create ads or newsletters or books or novels or screenplays or magazine articles or technical manuals or employee instructions.

The more *different* ways you apply it, the stronger your writing will become. The *faster* your writing will become.

And the more you'll remember it.

Every time you see the word "fast," let it help you write *fast*.

If you grasp this, lightning speed is within your reach.

Daily Pages

Here's a "secret" every professional writer knows.

You can't wait for the Muse to strike. You can't wait for inspiration.

Some days will be better than others. And, yes, inspiration is important. But you won't get anything on the page if you're not accustomed to writing.

So every day (including weekends and holidays), you must write something. *Anything*.

Call it your Daily Pages.

They can be pages from your book, or pages from a diary. They can be emails. Or web pages. Or newsletters.

And it's perfectly okay if they're the most awful, rancid, worthless piles of horse-pucky the world has ever known. Doesn't matter. As long as you write every single day.

Set a target for yourself. Start with one or two pages. But work your way up to *ten or more*. Aim to write *fast!*

And if you're working on a project (in the Apply phase or parts of the Strengthen phase), go ahead and count your pages.

Writers write.

Good writers write *often*.

I know you've heard all this stuff before. I'd heard it, too! But I never took it to heart. In fact, even when I was *teaching* this stuff, I didn't do it myself.

I do now. And it makes all the difference in the world.

It's one thing to *know* the FAST System. But until you write, it's all in your head. And that's not writing. That's *thinking*.

Write every single day.

As simple as it seems, if you only followed one piece of advice from this whole book, *this* is the tip I'd suggest.

Email

For me, Daily Pages are a normal part of life. Because in 1992, I became an internet geek.

I bought my first computer and plugged it into the wall. I played hundreds of hours of computer games.

Eventually, I figured out how to plug it into a *phone line*. It was a new thing called the "Internet," and it had text scrolling across the page at 1200 bits per second (yeah, way back *then!*).

The technology fascinated me.

I could connect my computer in North Hollywood, California to a computer in Johannesburg, South Africa, and instantly share information. I was floored! I couldn't believe it.

I started chatting on the internet, and participating in forums. And without even noticing, I began typing 80 words per minute.

And then I discovered email.

Email is Technology's *gift* to writers.

It's as if email was purpose-built to make writing easier.

Think about it. There's no pressure to be "good." You need to *write* them. You do it *daily*, so it's great typing practice.

Over the past three years alone, my "sent mail" folder says I've sent 6,578 emails (and I figure that's only about 70% of them — I delete a lot, too). And it's mid-April now, and I'm up to 965 already for this year.

When you write that much email, *you get faster at typing*.

Sure, you can shoot off one-word replies. But why not take the time to practice your writing skills? Why not *use* this tool every day to apply the FAST System?

Turn it into a habit. Make it your practice session.

Heck, make your *email* your Daily Pages! You'll stay in touch with friends and family, and it'll push you to find new and interesting things to write about.

If you're not using it — or not using it *enough* — you're missing out on one of today's greatest tools.

Use it. And whenever you do, apply the FAST System.

You'll get to "lightning speed" a whole lot quicker.

Hardwiring Your Brain

I saved this one for near-last.

It's the Payoff.

Remember the picture from chapter 4? The image of the brain we're always shown on documentaries? That mesh inside your head with electrical pulses pumping through it?

I want to show you how to use it — how to reach lightning speed by *manipulating* the mesh inside your brain.

It's pretty simple, really. Here's how it works.

Suppose you buy a lottery ticket every single week.

The first time you do it, you notice a big jackpot. *Aw, what the heck*, you think. You walk four blocks to the store. You plunk down five bucks. You get the quick-pick numbers. You wander home, and flick on the television set that night.

A little electrical pulse pumps through that mesh in your brain. It creates a memory. It's faint. And it's quickly forgotten. But it's there.

The next week, you think, *Maybe this week I'll get lucky*, and you do it again. The walk. The five bucks. The quick-pick. The walk back. The television.

The pulse pumps through the mesh — in the same spot. But now the mesh is twice as charged. The memory gets stronger.

The next week, you try again. Walk, buy, pick, walk, watch.

That electrical pulse digs into that mesh. Same spot again. That trip to the store is now etched into your brain.

And as week follows week, you do it again and again. That pulse is burning — *searing* — into the mesh.

You're forming a habit.

It's difficult to erase. Nearly impossible to forget. It's "second-nature" to you now. And before you know it, you're buying lottery tickets without even thinking.

Think about your life.

What actions are etched into your mind?

Are there certain television shows you watch every week? Do you take the same route to work each day? Do you tuck yourself into bed the same way each night? Do you greet people with the same words? Are there foods you eat regularly? Words you say repeatedly? Thoughts you play over and over again?

The mesh *is* the web of memories in your mind. And it's formed by what you do, how often you do it, and the impact *doing* it had on you.

It makes *bad* habits incredibly difficult to break.

But for us writers, we can *use* this!

Whatever you *want* to achieve, simply do it. Repeatedly.

If you apply the FAST System every day... If you write pages every single day... If you write *fast* every time you write...

...you'll be *hardwiring your brain!*

Writing *fast* becomes a ritual. A habit. You'll be training yourself to write better, faster and more effectively.

And all it requires is that you do it every single day.

When your brain is hardwired to write FAST, you will *always* write quickly. Gradually, you won't even have to *think* about it.

It's becomes second-nature.

That's just the way you write.

And I'll tell you something. It's better than any lottery ticket could ever be.

What is Lightning Speed Really?

So how fast *is* "lightning speed," and are you sure you've got it yet?

Lightning speed is a metaphor. It's not just a metaphor for "quick." Underneath that is a much larger metaphor.

Lightning speed is the *speed of thought*.

Your mind races at a blazing speed. Formulating ideas. Rejecting ideas. Connecting the dots. Controlling the workload. Working on puzzles from years ago.

Writing FAST is writing as close to the speed of thought as you can reach. *Your* speed. Of *your* thought.

And then reaching the reader — at *her* speed of thought.

The faster you write, the less you'll get in your own way. Stray ideas and distractions can't stop you, because you're directly in tune with your thought process.

The FAST System connects you with your own mind.

It lets you harness your mind. It lets you put what's *in* your mind directly onto the page.

And from the page, you touch the mind of your reader.

Ideas sparking ideas.

That is what writing at lightning speed is all about.

And so...

I started this book with a story. The story of the cavemen and the Mammoth. I'd like to finish with a story, too. And I'll take a little creative license here, as well.

Ooga had a great-grandfather named — I dunno — let's call him *Looga*.

One day (long before Ooga was even born), Looga was out wandering the countryside, collecting berries for winter.

Just as the sun was setting over the horizon, a storm rolled in. The clouds were deep and dark and threatened to downpour. Looga noticed it, and hurried back down the path to the cave.

But suddenly, the clouds started spitting bolts of lightning at the ground. Looga freaked. He'd heard crazy tales of these lightning bolts, and figured the gods were angry at him. He didn't think he'd done anything wrong, but now was no time to argue! He hid under a nearby tree.

It was getting dark, but it wasn't safe to keep going.

So, for half an hour, he sat terrified under that tree.

Suddenly, the giant spark of a stray bolt of lightning crashed down upon the tree above him. He shielded his head from the noise — and thought he was a dead man.

When it fell quiet again, he checked his bearskin coat, amazed. He was still intact. But when he looked up, Looga saw a curious sight.

The tree above him was dancing with a strange orange-and-red glow. He had never seen anything like it, and he watched in wonder. Transfixed.

Without warning, a branch snapped off the tree and slammed onto the ground, missing him by inches.

It sat there, at his feet — the orange-and-red glow flicking off the top of the branch. He reached out to touch it but — owww! — nearly burned his hand.

As the sky fell completely black, the tree and the area stayed lit. Thanks to this orange-and-red glow, Looga could see great distances, even at nighttime!

He grabbed the end of the branch that wasn't glowing, and held it above his head. The whole area was illuminated. It was as if daylight was still with him. He smiled.

Looga took his new torch safely through the night back to his cave. Another discovery had been made.

Ideas spark ideas.

And it all begins with one stray bolt of lightning.

66 Life is a challenge. **99**
Meet it.

—Anonymous

And So...

Wow.

I can't believe we made it.

Days of torture. Nights without sleep.

The confusion, the frustration, the insecurity — all leading to the point of exhaustion!

And that's just *you!* Imagine how *I've* felt!

(Insert canned laughter here.)

This book started out as a "framework" project.

As I was putting FASTscreenplay together, I realized it needed a *systematic* approach to writing. A foundation. A backbone. Next thing I know, I'm in the middle of *this* book, and pulling my hair out.

See, I never intended to write a book.

But the fact that I *have*, just goes to show you it's possible. I *know* me. I know what a *challenge* this has been for me.

And if *I* can do this, *you* can do it, too.

If you were interested enough to *find* this book — and you've read all the way to *this* point — I guarantee you've got what it takes to go a little further, and complete your own projects.

The FAST System was created for *you*. Not for those people who *say* they want to write. Not for anyone who *starts* this book and quits halfway through. And certainly not for the ones that *plan* to apply it, but never do.

No. It was written for *you* — that rare 5% that actually *does* something with it.

And I want to *make sure* you do something with it.

That's why I encourage feedback.

It's why I urge you to take it to the next level — and to help *me* take it to the next level. I want you to *apply* the FAST System and give me your real-world reactions to it.

Because the FAST System works. This book is *proof* of it.

But I know it can work even better.

More FAST to Come

I'll tell you something.

There's an incredible irony to this book.

It's a book on writing, but I never wanted to write it.

It's a book about a *system*, but I only *discovered* the system *as* I was writing the book *about* the system(!).

It's a book of advice, but I couldn't complete it until I followed the advice myself.

A funny thought occurred to me about halfway through:

"I should've written this book *after* I wrote this book!"

That would've made much more sense.

And that's why I consider this an *interactive* book. Think of it as "The FAST System, Version 1.0."

Ideas spark ideas. Hopefully mine spark yours. And with feedback, *yours* can spark *mine*, too.

If you're interested, I plan to release future editions of this book. To expand on FAST. To answer unanswered questions. To simplify anything that's unclear.

So let me know what you think!

Please visit **writingFAST.com/feedback** and share your reactions, your thoughts, your discoveries.

The Second Edition

The book you're reading now is the official First Edition. I hadn't planned to release it wide, but here it is.

Originally, the plan was this:

I'd launch *Writing FAST* as a Limited Edition book available only to subscribers of the Screenplay.com.au newsletter, and to people who happened to stumble across it on the Internet.

The goal was to get feedback on that Limited Edition, and

then *use* that feedback to shape the Second Edition. (I've got a ton of my own ideas for the Second Edition, but I want it to reflect what *readers* want — what *you* want!)

And then a funny thing happened.

The feedback from that Limited Edition was overwhelmingly positive! Maybe the book was better than I thought?

So, rather than use *only* my ideas for the Second Edition, I decided to release this First Edition, as is, even wider. To get more people to read it, and to provide feedback.

Look, I don't just want you to read this book.

I want you to *use* it!

And if you tell me how it might help *you* better, I can make the Second Edition even more powerful.

But I can't read your mind.

So by all means, *please* visit that link above, and send me your thoughts.

How can I improve it? Is there anything that isn't clear? Anything missing? Has it pushed you to action? If not, what *could* be added to help you get your work written fast?

A Word About My Teaching

As I wrote this book, I kept having one major difficulty — sharing with you the same passion, understanding, and level of *detail* as I would with my screenwriting workshops.

I've lived with the FAST System for about four months now.

And I think it's amazing.

But I've lived with screenwriting for about fifteen *years*.

So which do you think I'm better at teaching?

I've had to make this book somewhat generic.

See, in order for it to be useful for *any* kind of writing (even types of writing I have no interest in) I couldn't go into detail about the *one* subject I'm *most* passionate about:

Movies.

I couldn't use some of my favorite screenwriting examples. I couldn't even include some of the things I most enjoy teaching!

Simply because it's not appropriate to everyone.

So I hope you'll take the next step, and discover what I *really* want to share with you.

What I'm *passionate* about.

Beyond *Writing FAST*

Sure, the FAST System applies to *any* kind of writing.

But it was *created* for my screenwriting students. It was *developed* as a way to help them *apply* what I taught them in my screenwriting workshops.

It was meant to *enhance* all that other information. To tie everything together.

This book distilled the FAST System for *anyone*.

But FASTscreenplay takes it to the next level.

FASTscreenplay is the home study course I'm developing, which covers screenwriting from the *producer's* perspective.

And I'm excited about it, because it's a *complete* approach to writing screenplays — something I've spent four years perfecting.

In fact, even if you *don't* want to write screenplays, seeing how FAST applies to a specific *type* of writing, can help you better understand the system itself.

If you're interested, visit **FASTscreenplay.com** to learn more.

That's not meant to be a sales pitch. It's just an option.

And it's only *one* option.

No matter *what* you want to write, it's time to take the FAST System, and push it to the "next level."

And that means *applying* it.

Every kind of writing has its own unique requirements. I can help you with screenwriting. But if you're writing something else, *learn its requirements*. Understand them.

Take it to the next level by digging in and making it *work!*

You can do it. Let this book be the *start*, not the finish.

Final Thoughts

Before we depart, I want to close on this note.

I never considered myself a writer before. I've written some screenplays, some stories, and some articles — but all out of necessity. Writing was never my real focus.

So I don't want you to think this book is full of examples of great writing. It's decent, and it does the trick — but I know *you* can do better.

Heck, I know *I* can do better, now that I understand it!

It's been a learning experience for me, and I hope for you, too. If nothing else, take *this* away from this book:

Put yourself out there, and see what happens.

Yes, you open yourself up to judgement and criticism.

But you also spark ideas.

How many ideas will *this* book spark? How many books will you write? How many screenplays? News stories? Magazine articles? TV shows? Letters? Dissertations? Business plans? Websites? Ads? ...

All of them, I hope.

I've enjoyed writing this.

It's been painful and challenging. But I survived.

And because of that, I know *you* will, too.

That snickering woman from Chapter 2 might've had something right after all.

Apply the FAST System, and you'll see what I mean.

May *your* ideas spark many.

Perfect for new writers!

Beyond FAST:
11 Mistakes that Slow You Down

If you have purchased this book through a bookstore, you might not realize that *Writing FAST* has a companion audio seminar on CD, called:

Beyond FAST: 11 Mistakes that Slow You Down

Join Jeff, as he leaves the classroom to take you on a journey *through* eleven of the biggest mistakes that slow writers down.

Take the FAST System to the next level, and discover simple, easy-to-apply solutions that help you correct those mistakes immediately, and write faster than ever before.

And this is no ordinary audio seminar. In one richly-illustrated hour, you'll go to the beach, the snow, the city, the country, and more. You'll even go to the past — and to the future — as the solutions become clear!

Plus, you'll also look at four techniques for making your writing electrifying. And to top it off, there's a special *bonus* segment, too — a walk-through of the Talktation technique!

Beyond FAST goes well and truly beyond what you're expecting, and becomes a valuable resource — and an entertaining ride — you'll refer to again and again.

Simply visit **http://writingFAST.com** for complete instructions on how to get your copy of this powerful CD... at an enormous discount!

About the Author

Jeff Bollow is an award-winning L.A.-born filmmaker, currently living in Sydney, Australia. With a career spanning twenty years, three countries, and every facet of the film industry, Jeff has worked on feature films (from major Hollywood movies to tiny independent films), as well as television, TV commercials, music videos, theatre, industrial films, educational projects, and documentary productions.

As the founder of Screenplay.com.au (a resource created to help Australian screenwriters write and sell commercially-viable material), Jeff is a highly-regarded teacher, known for his passion, and the breadth of his knowledge.

He aims to create an independent feature film studio capable of producing three to six films per year. The FAST System and all screenwriting efforts have evolved out of his need for material.

His one hope is that his students will *write*.

Writing FAST is his first book.

The FAST System Step-by-Step

Focus YOUR IDEA

1. Capture it

See what you've got
Look beyond the obvious
Brainstorm a new list of ideas
Take it to its conclusion
Write it down in one single sentence

2. Make it specific

Consider your idea
Make it tangible
Test your approach
Flesh it out
Create your Preview

3. Create your plan

Decide on your end result
Determine the page count
Divide it into chunks
Flesh out each level's details
Add booster areas

Apply YOUR PLAN

1. Speed writing/Talktation

Plant the idea in your head
Match your thought to your typing
Talk your words onto the page
Increase your thought speed
Practice, and practice some more

2. Harness the overflow

Fix on the goal
Notice the stray idea
Drop it in the BIN
Shut it out and keep going
Review your ideas later

3. Ride the wave

Determine your checkpoint
Jump on the wave
Don't think
Find your speed zone
Enjoy

TWEAK YOUR WORDS

Sharpen the speed

Re-read refreshed
Take the ride
Find the missing impact points
Fill and tighten
Create a Speed Plan

Command attention

Zoom in
See the richness
Question everything
Earn their interest
Adjust the Speed Plan

Quicken and polish

Touch each word
Watch like a hawk
Apply the Speed Plan
Let go
Give it to your reader

STRENGTHEN YOUR WRITING

Inspect your work

Put yourself in the reader's shoes
Read it through completely
Write down your thoughts
Re-read and make notes
Create your Problem List

Decide which way to go

Review your Problem List
Apply the Stack Test
Grade each element
Prioritize the results
Create your Strengthen Plan

Amplify your writing

Prepare to work quickly
Re-Focus for clarity
Research for detail
Edit for impact
One notch at a time

More Information

This book has been created to help you write — *fast*.
But it doesn't exist in a vacuum.
In fact, we've been helping writers generate commercially-viable screenplays in Australia since early 2000.
For more information, visit any of the websites below.
We're here to help!

writingFAST.com

Information about the FAST System, and ordering, press, trade and feedback for this book — *Writing FAST: How to Write Anything with Lightning Speed*.

FASTscreenplay.com

Information, ordering, press, trade and feedback for *FASTscreenplay*, the breakthrough new home study screenwriting course.

Screenplay.com.au

Australia's Screenplay Development Centre offers a wide range of screenwriting-related services, including workshops, professional software, evaluations, coverage, script editing, mentorships, and more.

embryo-films.com/publishing

The new publishing arm of Embryo Films. *Writing FAST* is our debut title, with additional products coming soon.

Notes

Notes

Notes

Notes